SOUTH ASIA SUBREGIONAL
ECONOMIC COOPERATION

OPERATIONAL PLAN
2016–2025 UPDATE

Notes:
In this publication, "$" refers to United States dollars.
ADB recognizes "Ceylon" as Sri Lanka, "China" as the People's Republic of China, and "Korea" as the Republic of Korea.

Cover design by Cleone Baradas.

CONTENTS

TABLES AND MAPS

TABLES

MAPS

FOREWORD

The member countries of the South Asia Subregional Economic Cooperation (SASEC) Program—Bangladesh, Bhutan, India, Maldives, Myanmar, Nepal, and Sri Lanka—have increasingly turned to regional cooperation in order to sustain growth and realize the subregion's economic potential. Considered as one of the fastest growing subregions in Asia, SASEC, while blessed with rich natural and demographic resources, faces various development challenges, such as poverty, inadequate infrastructure, and policy inefficiencies, as well as threats of natural disasters and climate change.

In 2016, the SASEC countries adopted the SASEC Operational Plan (OP) 2016–2025, as the program's first comprehensive medium- to long-term plan to build on the SASEC program's achievements since 2001. The SASEC OP expands the scope of regionally-oriented investments, more closely aligned with development thrusts of individual SASEC countries through refocused strategies in transport, trade facilitation, and energy, and new focus on economic corridor development. To further realize gains from SASEC collaboration, SASEC finance ministers adopted a vision of *SASEC: Powering Asia in the 21st Century* in April 2017 in New Delhi, India. The vision calls for leveraging opportunities and synergies among three levers—natural resources, industry potential, and connectivity—to maximize the benefits from regional economic cooperation.

Following these two key SASEC milestones, the SASEC portfolio has grown from 41 projects worth $8.27 billion in 2016, to 55 projects worth $12.53 billion by end of August 2019. Asian Development Bank (ADB) financing for SASEC projects during this period has grown from $4.85 billion to $7.23 billion. Additional developments necessitated updating the SASEC OP. Member countries have called for rationalizing the project pipeline, confirming what constitutes SASEC projects based on existing and planned transport and energy networks in the subregion, and enhancing the trade facilitation strategic framework. They also expressed the need to better screen projects based on their preparedness and funding possibilities.

With the valuable inputs of the member countries, ADB has conducted a comprehensive stock take of completed and ongoing projects financed by SASEC governments, ADB, and other development partners. Future projects were then assessed as to their roles in filling the "gaps" that countries need to work on to complete the SASEC networks.

The result is a more streamlined SASEC OP, which now constitutes 111 proposed projects with financing requirements of about $58.71 billion, with transport leading the way in terms of the number (76) and cost of projects ($39.15 billion). Further screening for preparedness in terms of identified financing further trims the pipeline to 77 projects with financing of $45.65 billion.

This updated SASEC OP is envisaged to spur the interest of member governments and development partners in considering SASEC projects in their programming discussions. ADB, as SASEC secretariat, will continue to work closely with the member countries in updating and refining the SASEC OP to maximize its contribution to attaining the SASEC Vision's goals of multimodal connectivity, energy market development, and increased trade.

Hun Kim
Director General, South Asia Department
Asian Development Bank

I SOUTH ASIA SUBREGIONAL ECONOMIC COOPERATION OVERVIEW

1   The South Asia Subregional Economic Cooperation (SASEC) Program brings together Bangladesh, Bhutan, India, Maldives, Myanmar, Nepal, and Sri Lanka in a project-based partnership to promote regional prosperity by improving cross-border connectivity, facilitating faster and less costly trade among participating countries, and strengthening regional economic cooperation.[1] The Asian Development Bank (ADB) is the Secretariat and lead financier and development partner of SASEC, which has simple institutional arrangements, but heavy on projects that comprise it. Its institutional mechanism consists of annual nodal officials' meetings for setting strategic directions, and regular meetings of SASEC working groups and subgroups to review progress and agree on future work plans. The program helps achieve improved cross-border connectivity and increased intra-subregional trade using a pragmatic, flexible, multitrack, multispeed, and results-oriented initiative focused on transport, trade facilitation, and energy.

2   Results in these areas have been substantial: (i) in transport, the emphasis on improving international corridor segments, combined with better border facilities, has helped expand trade and commerce; (ii) in trade facilitation, efforts focused on modernizing and harmonizing customs operations, improving border facilities, and facilitating through-transport, thus helping reduce constraints to trade; and (iii) in energy, improving cross-border power transmission connectivity has helped harness clean hydropower to meet demand in the subregion and, overall, raised the level of energy security and reliability in the subregion.

3   As of December 2018, the SASEC portfolio amounted to around $11.36 billion for 52 projects covering the transport and energy sectors, economic corridor development, trade facilitation, and information and communication technology.[2] Transport is the largest sector with 34 projects costing $9.10 billion, followed by energy with 12 projects at $1.50 billion. Of the total cost, ADB has contributed almost $6.60 billion, while SASEC governments and other cofinanciers have contributed over $4.80 billion.

---

[1]   The SASEC program has covered Bangladesh, Bhutan, India, and Nepal since 2001, and expanded to include Maldives and Sri Lanka in 2014, and Myanmar in 2017.

[2]   Loan 3716-SRI: SASEC Port Access Elevated Highway, which will provide a direct link to the city center and the port from Colombo–Katunayake Expressway via New Kelani Bridge, is not included in the list even if approved in September 2018 since it was committed only in January 2019.

THE SOUTH ASIA SUBREGIONAL ECONOMIC COOPERATION OPERATIONAL PLAN 2016–2025

4   The SASEC Operational Plan (OP) 2016–2025, adopted by SASEC members in May 2016, involves a refocusing of operational priorities as reflected in an updated pipeline of projects in key sectors and areas of cooperation, namely transport, trade facilitation, energy, and economic corridor development (ECD). Refocusing of priorities involves, among others, expanding transport and trade facilitation efforts in maritime cooperation, extending energy cooperation in renewable energy and energy efficiency, and adding ECD as a priority area of cooperation. The SASEC OP has provided a rolling pipeline of over 200 potential priority projects requiring over $120.00 billion in investments.[3]

5   The strategic objectives of the SASEC OP are as follows:

(a)   Enhancing physical connectivity through multimodal transport systems that are aligned more closely with the development of markets

(b)   Following a comprehensive approach to transport and trade facilitation that will expand the current focus to include seaborne facilitation, to complement investments in multimodal networks

(c)   Enhancing electricity trade and expanding and diversifying energy supply to meet energy needs and secure power reliability, and

(d)   Promoting synergies between economic corridors being developed in individual SASEC countries and optimizing development impacts of economic corridor investments through improved cross-border links

6   **The SASEC Vision.** The first SASEC Finance Ministers' Meeting, held in New Delhi, India, in April 2017, launched the SASEC Vision document—*SASEC: Powering Asia in the 21st Century*. The SASEC Vision document provides the comprehensive blueprint to transform the subregion into Asia's growth engine in the 21st century, by tapping synergies that leverage resource-based industries, expand regional value chains, and strengthen gateways and hubs between and among the countries. Investments and activities under the SASEC OP—designed to achieve seamless transport connectivity, more efficient trade processes, stronger energy trade infrastructure, and more economically vibrant transport corridors—will serve as the foundation for achieving the SASEC Vision.

---

3   Various meetings were held from 2013 to 2015, identified the list of projects in the original SASEC OP which included (i) Bay of Bengal Initiative for Multi-Sectoral Technical and Economic Cooperation (BIMSTEC) meetings to review the BIMSTEC Transport Infrastructure and Logistics Study (BTILS) Update held in 2013–2014; (ii) Meetings of Transport Secretaries of Bangladesh, Bhutan, India, and Nepal (BBIN) to prepare the BBIN Motor Vehicles Agreement signed in Thimphu, Bhutan, in June 2015; and (iii) the SASEC 2025 Regional Consultation Workshop held in Singapore in October 2015.

7 **Transport.** Transport remains SASEC's centerpiece, but with more focus on realizing seamless movement between intermodal transport systems along key trade routes. Its operational priorities are as follows:

(a) Road Transport: The aim is to upgrade and expand the road network along major trade routes, with measures covering (i) upgrade of key routes to Asian Highway Class I standards, (ii) upgrade of road links to primary SASEC routes and key borders, and (iii) upgrade of access roads to borders and ports to address "last mile" connectivity

(b) Railway: The aim is to improve connectivity, focusing on (i) enhanced railway connections between Bangladesh and India, (ii) improved connectivity with landlocked countries and the northeast region of India and to seaports, and (iii) enhanced connectivity between ports and their hinterlands

(c) Maritime Transport: The focus is on (i) developing deepwater ports for larger, deeper drafted vessels, and (ii) reducing port dwell times by augmenting port operating efficiency and enhancing container handling equipment in ports

(d) Inland Waterways: The objective is to promote coastal shipping and inland water transport to handle international trade, and

(e) Airports: The aim is to expand capacity to handle both passenger and airfreight traffic, as a result of growth in tourism and global value chains

8 **Trade Facilitation.** The SASEC OP extends the time horizon of the original SASEC Trade Facilitation Strategic Framework (2014–2018) and elevates the practices and processes of border clearance to international best practices. The operational priorities are as follows:

(a) Simplify trade documentation, increase automation, and expedite border clearance procedures to facilitate the movement of goods and vehicles: Priority will be given to reduce the overall number of trade documents, apply advanced procedures and practices based on international standards/conventions, and the use of advanced customs information technology (IT) systems to improve trade efficiency

(b) Promote automation in border agencies and facilitate development of national single windows (NSWs): The focus is on promoting automation in border agencies (to enable them to progressively link into an NSW), and in developing an NSW

(c) Strengthen national conformance bodies and develop infrastructure and facilities in sanitary and phytosanitary-related and other border agencies: This will help the countries to trade more efficiently in goods subject to sanitary and phytosanitary–technical barriers to trade measures and improve their access to markets in the region and globally

(d) Develop and implement through-transport motor vehicles agreements: This will aid the seamless movement of cargo and people in the region and reduce the levels of border transshipment

(e) Develop trade-related infrastructure in SASEC ports, land border crossings, and bonded logistics facilities adjacent to land borders and major centers of trade: The development of such infrastructure would improve process efficiency and regulatory effectiveness, and

(f) Build capacity and enhance cooperation and coordination mechanisms among stakeholders in trade facilitation

9   **Energy.** The focus on improving energy trade infrastructure and developing the regional power market was in response to the need to ease supply constraints and diversify the energy mix of SASEC countries. Complementing these are efforts to develop low-carbon alternatives and energy efficiency and conservation measures. The operational priorities for energy are as follows:

    (a)   Improve interconnections to access large-scale electricity and natural gas resources

    (b)   Harness unutilized regional indigenous hydropower potential

    (c)   Develop low-carbon energy (wind and solar), and

    (d)   Facilitate bilateral and regional coordination mechanisms and knowledge sharing (e.g., technology transfer development practices toward the regional power trade market)

Regional power interconnection arrangements and bilateral hydrocarbon trade have also been identified as flagship initiatives in the SASEC Vision document.

10   **Economic Corridor Development.** ECD involves leveraging of infrastructure connectivity to unlock the full potential of markets. National corridors have initially been identified as having potential synergies with other in-country corridors in the subregion. Under the SASEC OP, the objective is to promote better linkages between these in-country corridors to generate synergies for larger regional impact, with a focus on

    (a)   Reinforcing existing value chains and developing new value-chain linkages between in-country corridors

    (b)   Upgrading key transport and trade facilitation infrastructure to improve connectivity between in-country corridors, and

    (c)   Designing appropriate institutional mechanisms to serve as platforms for coordination and collaboration among governments and various stakeholders

III THE 2018-2019 PRIORITIZATION EXERCISE

11   Following the 2017 update of the SASEC Operational Plan 2016–2025, the Meeting of SASEC Nodal Officials and Working Groups, held in Singapore on 5–6 March 2018, requested that the projects in the SASEC OP be prioritized and sequenced, considering availability of financing and detailed project reports (DPRs). In this regard, ADB consulted the SASEC countries, and obtained a revised list of projects for prioritization. However, the resulting SASEC OP list remains long; regional cooperation and integration rationale for many of these projects was not clear; and information on project preparedness and funding availability was not firm. For these reasons, ADB felt that a more rigorous exercise of identification and prioritization of projects needed to be undertaken, in order to produce a credible list of committed and potential projects for the SASEC OP.

12   ADB came up with a revised process of SASEC OP Updating and Enhancement, which consisted of the following steps:

(a)   **Defining what are the SASEC projects that form part of the SASEC transport and electricity networks.**

For transport, the SASEC network of road and railway corridors, airports, and seaports was developed based on relevant existing studies and frameworks (e.g., South Asian Association for Regional Cooperation [SAARC] regional multimodal transport strategy, Bay of Bengal Initiative for Multi-Sectoral Technical and Economic Cooperation [BIMSTEC] transport infrastructure and logistics study, Asian Highway, Trans-Asian Railway, and internal ADB studies that defined the transport network). Relevant base maps developed for the four transport subsectors for the BIMSTEC transport network provide the basis for the SASEC transport network, specifically for the road and railway subsectors.

For energy, projects in the SASEC power transmission master plan study that was completed in 2016 had served as the universe of SASEC power projects. In the hydrocarbon subsector, the projects considered were those identified in the SASEC Vision document (liquefied natural gas [LNG] and liquefied petroleum gas [LPG] hubs). A base map of the power interconnection schemes that was identified in the master plan study was updated and produced.

For trade facilitation, SASEC projects are well defined in the SASEC Trade Facilitation Strategic Framework, which is actively being discussed and pursued by the SASEC trade facilitation working group and customs subgroup.

(b)   **Conducting a comprehensive stocktake on completed and ongoing regional cooperation and integration projects financed by ADB, other development partners, and SASEC governments.**

The stocktake used the information on ADB-supported SASEC projects, as well as SASEC projects funded by other development partners. It also used information generated from ongoing studies such as the BIMSTEC Transport Connectivity Master Plan.

For transport, locations of completed and ongoing projects were checked in relation to the SASEC road and railway corridor maps developed in step (a). A similar exercise was done for power projects. For trade facilitation projects, information on the initiatives being supported by other development partners is on hand, given ADB's strong working relationship with these partners.

(c) **Identifying future projects with existing/planned DPRs, relating these to the SASEC network base maps, and determining the "gaps" based on analysis of the maps and other information on projects.**

The SASEC secretariat undertook careful analysis of the list of planned SASEC transport and energy projects (with DPRs) that were obtained from the countries, and in consultation with ADB sector divisions, identified those with indicative funding commitment. The "gaps" in the SASEC transport and power networks were then identified.

IV THE SASEC OPERATIONAL PLAN PRIORITY PROJECTS

A. TRANSPORT

13   Priority transport projects were selected based on their respective roles in key sections of the existing multimodal transport networks that link important transport and trade nodes in the member countries. Development of transport connectivity under the SASEC OP was intended to address modal development needs more holistically, enhancing connectivity to promote economic development in the areas along the routes, as well as linking the main industrial centers (cities) and key transport nodes (ports and strategic logistical centers). The identification of important potential corridors was also based on routes selected by SAARC as being included as one of their road or railway corridors, to ensure an element of compatibility in regional initiatives. In addition, the countries should have development plans agreed to upgrade part or all of the particular corridor within their country. These plans need to have been included and published in national, SAARC, or other regional initiatives or development partner programs. Given that the initial focus is on short- and medium-term "win–win" development, significant enhancement programs on key sections of the corridor should be scheduled for start of implementation by 2025 at the latest. The selected SASEC priority transport projects consist of a combination of the main road and railway corridors and the intermodal nodes—ports and airports, which should lead to more effective economic corridor development.

14   **Road Transport.** Road transport is the dominant form of surface transport throughout the region and, consequently, it is the principal driver in identifying economic corridor potential. The key component of the development strategy is to upgrade corridor roads to Asian Highway (AH) Class I (dual carriageway) wherever the terrain allows and to Class II single carriageway in hilly and mountainous areas. The focus for the road subsector therefore, which remains the largest in terms of the number and value of projects, is on upgrading the quality and capacity of the national road network and its multimodal and cross-border connectivity. Following the proposed SASEC OP updating process described in paragraph 12(a), the following routes have been recognized as the key SASEC road transport corridors whose development will have a major influence on transport and trade costs between member states:

(i)   SASEC Road Corridor 1: The "Nepal–Kolkata Trade Corridor": Kathmandu–Birgunj/Raxaul–Kolkata/Haldia. This is the key trade route linking landlocked Nepal with its largest trading partner, India, as well as for trade with third countries passing through Kolkata Port or Haldia Port. On the Nepalese section, the potential to develop beyond AH Classification[4] Class II is limited north of the Terai plains. In India, most of the corridor is already dual carriageway, and thus the emphasis is on 4-laning the remaining Class II sections;

---

[4]   The Asian Highway classification and design standards provide the minimum standards and guidelines for the construction, improvement, and maintenance of Asian Highway routes. Source: Intergovernmental Agreement on the Asian Highway Network. https://www.unescap.org/sites/default/files/AH%20Agreement%20with%20 Amended%20Annex%20I-%202018_En.pdf (accessed 17 November 2019).

(ii)   SASEC Road Corridor 2: The "Bay of Bengal Highway" Thoothukudi (Tuticorin)–Chennai–Visakhapatnam–Kolkata–Dhaka–Chattogram (formerly Chittagong)–Cox's Bazar, with spurs Akhaura–Agartala and Bariarhat–Ramgarh–Sabroom. This consists initially of the important Indian East Coast Economic Corridor, which links all the Indian SASEC ports. This is almost all AH Class I, but the north and east of Kolkata becomes the key route for trade between SASEC's largest member states. Despite high traffic volumes, this important section remains AH Class II. On the Bangladesh side, the construction of the new Padma Multipurpose Bridge and the construction of newly aligned approach roads will have a significant impact on transport and trade costs between the two countries. These developments will provide an AH Class I route to Dhaka when completed. At the eastern end, the link between Dhaka and Chattogram carries 70% of Bangladesh's international trade. This section is predominantly AH Class I, but may need support with a parallel expressway, given the volume of freight traffic in particular;

(iii)   SASEC Road Corridor 3: The "India–Association of Southeast Asian Nations (ASEAN) East–West Corridor": Kolkata–Siliguri–Guwahati–Imphal–Moreh/Tamu–Mandalay–Bago–Myawaddy, with spurs Hasimara–Phuentsholing–Thimphu and Bago–Yangon. This is an important trade route for landlocked Bhutan and eastern Nepal, and connects with "India's East–West Corridor" that links the northeastern states of India with the rest of the country. With the connection farther east via the "Trilateral Highway," which links India, Myanmar, and Thailand, the corridor offers land-based connectivity between South Asia and Southeast Asia. At this stage, only limited sections are AH Class I, and mountainous terrain in southeast and southwest Myanmar will limit development to AH Class II;

(iv)   SASEC Road Corridor 4: The "Nepal/Bhutan–Bangladesh North–South Corridor": Kathmandu–Kakarvitta/Panitanki–Rangpur–Bogra–Dhaka–Chattogram, with spurs Rangpur–Burimari/Changrabandha–Phuentsholing, Bogra–Mongla, and Dhaka–Payra Port. This links landlocked Bhutan and Nepal with Bangladesh and enhances both their potential links to Bangladesh ports, as well as better trade access from the northwest of Bangladesh to these ports. Most roads are AH Class II, but extensive transition to AH Class I is planned in Bangladesh;

(v)   SASEC Road Corridor 5: The "North Bangladesh–India Connector": Dhaka–Sylhet–Tamabil–Dawki–Shillong–Guwahati, with spur Sylhet–Sheola–Karimganj–Silchar. This links central and northeastern Bangladesh with the northeastern states of India to promote both bilateral trade and links in the northeast to the "Trilateral Highway" and the Bangladesh ports in the south. This route is almost exclusively AH Class II but is scheduled for upgrading to dual carriageway in both countries; and

(vi)   SASEC Road Corridor 6: The "Sri Lanka Port Highway": Colombo–Dambulla–Trincomalee, with spur Kurunegala–Kandy. This is designed to enhance connectivity between the main port in Colombo with its northern hinterland, as well as with its main port in the northeast of the island closest to neighboring India. Currently, the route is all AH Class II but is scheduled to be gradually upgraded to four lanes.

15   Map 1 is the schematic map of the routes of the six road corridors. Meanwhile, Appendix 1 details the projects under each of the six corridors. Appendix 5 details all transport projects in each country.

Map 1: SASEC Road Corridors

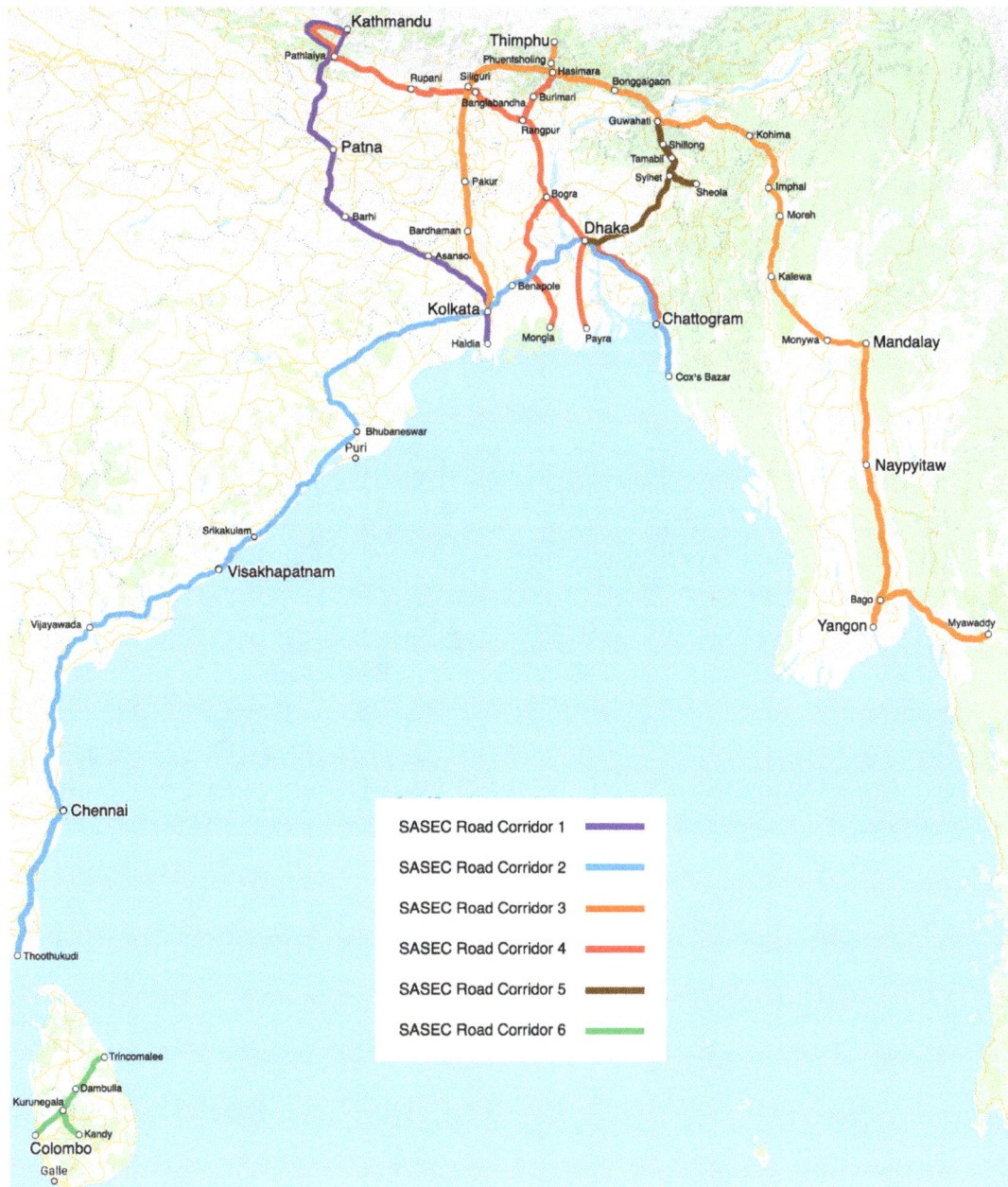

SASEC = South Asia Subregional Economic Cooperation.

Note: The boundaries, colors, denominations, and any other information shown on the map do not imply, on the part of the Asian Development Bank, any judgment on the legal status of any territory, or any endorsement or acceptance of such boundaries, colors, denominations, or information.

Source: Asian Development Bank.

Note that, for several priority road projects for Bangladesh, the feasibility studies and detailed engineering designs were completed under ADB technical assistance. In Bhutan, priority projects will (i) upgrade cross-border connectivity corridors for enhanced logistics and trade; (ii) expand the national road network to better connect remote areas, especially the eastern regions, and open them up for better economic opportunities; and (iii) include improving road linkages with inland ports.

In India, roads along major SASEC trade routes, which provide access to borders and ports, will be upgraded mostly with government funding under the Bharatmala Program, an umbrella program for the road sector that focuses on optimizing efficiency of road traffic movement across the country.[5] In Myanmar, SASEC road projects align exclusively with the Trilateral Highway, which connect to Thailand. In Nepal, priority road projects will upgrade the strategic road network and improve links between remote areas and key trade routes and gateways. The expressway network in Sri Lanka will be upgraded for better mobility between regions and the sea and air gateways, reducing congestion in critical sections.

16   **Railway.** In addition to the above road corridors, there are two important railway corridors that form part of the SASEC transport network, complementing SASEC Road Corridors 1 and 2:

(i)   SASEC Railway Corridor 1: "Nepal–Kolkata Trade Corridor": Birgunj–Raxaul–Muzaffarpur–Patna–Gaya–Asansol–Kolkata–Haldia, which links landlocked Nepal with the Indian ports and is particularly important for containerized import traffic. In addition, much of the bilateral bulk traffic between the two countries uses this route, which suffers some congestion, particularly near Kolkata, limiting the availability of train paths.

(ii)   SASEC Railway Corridor 2: "India–Bangladesh Rail Corridor": Kolkata–Ranaghat–Gede–Tangail–Dhaka–Cumilla–Chattogram (Chittagong)–Cox's Bazar, including spur lines 2A: Cumilla–Agartala–Akhaura, 2B: links to northwest Bangladesh, 2C: Darshana–Khulna–Mongla, and 2D: connections to Payra Port. At this corridor's western half is the major route for bilateral movement of bulk traffic between India and Bangladesh (Gede–Darshana), while the eastern half is important in both (i) linking Dhaka with its main port (e.g., Chattogram) and extension to Cox's Bazar, and (ii) bilateral connection through the Agartala–Akhaura link under development.

17   Map 2 is the schematic map of the routes of the two railway corridors. Meanwhile, Appendix 2 details the projects under each of the two railway corridors, while Appendix 5 details the transport projects by country. In Bangladesh, railway projects will develop railway links to connect to India and ensure gauge compatibility. Railway and inland river transport projects are designed to link ports (Mongla and Chattogram seaports) to Bhutan, Nepal, and northeast India for international trade purposes. Upgrading of India's railway links with neighbors (Bangladesh and Nepal) is handled by India's Ministry of Railways.

18   **Ports.** All the SASEC main ports are located along the SASEC transport corridors, being key transport nodes along at least one of the SASEC road corridors, and, in most cases, being on one of the two railway corridors. The development focus is principally on upgrading port capacity to handle container growth and handling performance.

---

5   Several road projects in Assam were identified by ADB's Joghigopa multimodal logistics parks study as part of the government's recent focus on improving the efficiency of the logistics sector. These projects will provide better links to other SASEC countries while integrating India's northeastern region with the domestic market.

Map 2: Proposed SASEC Railway Corridors

SASEC = South Asia Subregional Economic Cooperation.

Note: The boundaries, colors, denominations and any other information shown on the map do not imply, on the part of the Asian Development Bank, any judgment on the legal status of any territory, or any endorsement or acceptance of such boundaries, colors, denominations or information.

Source: Asian Development Bank.

19   Appendix 3 details the port projects by country. In India, port development (new and upgrade) will provide needed capacity for larger vessels and container trade. India emphasizes port-led industrialization under the Sagarmala Initiative, capitalizing on its strategic location in maritime routes and global production networks.[6] Several agreements and protocols have been signed between India and its neighbors to develop the regional network. In Sri Lanka, regional port development will support industrial development in identified districts through lower transport costs. Colombo port investments will help meet the demand for container transshipment and related logistics businesses for the international market.

---

[6]   This also reinforces ADB's commitment to economic corridor development especially the East Coast Economic Corridor, which aims to invigorate the eastern region's manufacturing activity and integrate it with the vibrant production networks in Asia.

20 **Airports.** The main SASEC airports are also located along the SASEC transport corridors. The development focus is mainly on upgrading passenger terminals to address predicted growth in passenger traffic, particularly that being generated by low-cost carriers, and additional runways, taxiways, and aprons to handle larger aircrafts.

21 Appendix 4 details the airport projects by country. In Bhutan, the airport project aims to upgrade infrastructure, security, and facilities at secondary airports to increase air connectivity, enhance the movement of people and goods, as well as to boost the tourism sector. In Nepal, airport investments will upgrade the main gateway and alternative airports for increased tourism.

B. TRADE FACILITATION

22 The focus of the operational priorities under trade facilitation is to make trade more efficient in the region, reducing the cost and time taken for cross-border flow of cargo, adopting international standards, improving compliance, and supporting the sector through capacity building and coordination mechanisms for sustainable implementation. ADB technical assistance will conduct necessary studies to aid in the implementation. Appendix 6 contains more information on trade facilitation projects.

23 The key country-wise features of the trade facilitation priority pipeline are as follows:

(a) Bangladesh: In support of customs modernization efforts, a possible policy-based loan (PBL) to the Government of Bangladesh amounting to about $48.00 million is under discussion. The PBL will promote reforms related to the implementation of the World Trade Organization (WTO) Trade Facilitation Agreement (TFA) and will be a follow-on assistance to the SASEC Trade Facilitation Program PBL, approved in September 2012. The outputs of the possible PBL are as follows: (i) customs legal and regulatory framework aligned with international standards and other best practices; (ii) cargo clearance processes made more efficient, predictable, transparent, and automated; and (iii) trade infrastructure for effective functioning of customs strengthened. Capacity-building support will be rendered for the introduction of modern techniques and for the development of specialized centers under the National Board of Revenue.

The priority projects for Bangladesh will also include the development and upgrading of infrastructural facilities and connectivity links at select border crossing points, and implementation of trade facilitation reforms in a coordinated manner. A project loan for developing the land customs stations and integrated border management facilities at selected border crossing points, procurement of scanners, automation of operations establishing a central customs laboratory in Dhaka, and associated capacity building is also under discussion with the Government of Bangladesh. A dry port would be developed at Tongi–Joydevpur to facilitate off-border clearance of cargo.

(b) Bhutan: A national single window (NSW) would be developed as a single electronic platform for conducting processes related to international trade. This would assist the private sector in the efficient operation of their trade activities, reducing duplication in compliance work and expediting the release of cargo.

(c)   India: Integrated check posts at selected land borders with Bangladesh, Bhutan, and Nepal will be developed by India using its own resources. This project will entail comprehensive development of infrastructure at the identified border points to cater to the needs of all cross-border regulatory agencies and private traders. Technical assistance will be provided for building awareness of global standards and best practices in trade and transport facilitation to assist in the implementation of the WTO TFA and tools of the World Customs Organization.

(d)   Maldives: The priority project for Maldives is to establish the NSW project to integrate all the border agencies on a single electronic platform and ensure fast and efficient goods clearance. Project preparatory work commenced in May 2018. Maldives will also strengthen its national quality infrastructure system to facilitate the removal of unnecessary technical barriers to trade and increase the marketability and integrity of Maldives' products and services in international markets.

(e)   Myanmar: The focus of trade facilitation sector projects for Myanmar would be to assist in implementing the WTO TFA, through capacity building in areas such as (i) advance rulings, (ii) publication of average release times, (iii) freedom of transit, (iv) customs cooperation, and (v) NSW.

(f)   Sri Lanka: ADB is providing technical assistance (piggybacked to Loan 3716-SRI-SASEC Port Access Elevated Highway) to support the country's trade logistics and optimize improved port connectivity through (i) improvements in risk management system, and (ii) improvements in inland cargo clearance system through off-dock facilities and the use of electronic cargo tracking system to secure cargo during transit.

C. ENERGY

24   **Status of Regional Power Trade.** Rapid economic development and the urgency toward attaining 100% electrification in countries, such as India and Bangladesh, have resulted in rapid growth in demand for power in the SASEC subregion. This then translates into greater emphasis in meeting reliable and stable power supply, particularly in a country like Bangladesh where alternative power generation sources are needed to diversify supply and augment constrained traditional energy sources. The SASEC Vision includes subregional power trade as one of its flagship initiatives, as it can provide cheaper renewable power (mainly hydropower) from Bhutan and Nepal to power-consuming Bangladesh, India, and Sri Lanka. This can also enable power swap arrangements to meet seasonal variations in power demand and supply.

25   SASEC power exchange is currently taking place with India in bilateral trade arrangement individually with Bangladesh, Bhutan, Nepal, and Myanmar. India is a natural center for SASEC power exchange, given India's central geographic location, large generation capacity and huge demand, and whose transmission system is operated as a synchronous national grid (at 50 hertz). Following the SAARC Kathmandu declaration on energy trading (in November 2014) and feedback from the regional countries on the Guidelines on Cross Border Electricity issued by India's Ministry of Power in December 2016, India released its revised guidelines in December 2018 covering (i) tripartite trading

of electricity through agreements for transmission corridor access, (ii) trading through power exchanges after clearances from designated authorities, and (iii) easing of restrictions on ownership for export and import of power.

(a)   India–Bhutan Trade

26   Since 1986, Bhutan has been a net exporter of hydropower to India through the following: (i) 336-megawatt (MW) Chukha hydropower plant (HPP) via 220-kilovolt (kV) lines to Birpara, India; (ii) 60 MW Kurichhu HPP (from 2001 to 2002) via the 132 kV Gelephu–Salakati (Assam) and Motanga–Rangia lines; and (iii) 1,020 MW Tala HPP (starting 2006–2007) via two 400 kV lines (at Khogla and Pagli). These lines are used for Bhutan's power imports of 20 MW–30 MW during the winter season. The associated transmission system to bring power to the desired load center is incorporated in each new HPP developed in Bhutan.

27   There are three ongoing HPPs for export to India: (i) 1,200 MW Punatsangchhu I, (ii) 1,020 MW Punatsangchhu II, and (iii) 720 MW Mangdechhu. Mangdechhu was expected to be commissioned by the end of February 2019, while commissioning was delayed for Punatsangchhu I (to 2022) and Punatsangchhu II (to 2019). The transmission lines to evacuate output of these HPPs are as follows:

- Punatsangchhu I: Two 400 kV lines—one to Lhamoizingkha border and another to Alipurduar high voltage direct current (HVDC) power pooling point in West Bengal;
- Punatsangchhu II: One 400 kV line to Jigmeling power pooling point; and
- Mangdechhu: Two 400 kV lines—one to Jigmeling pooling point and another to Alipurduar.

(b)   India–Nepal Trade

28   Power exchange between India and Nepal is based on the principle of catering to the power needs of isolated local border areas of Nepal. Power is supplied to the Nepal Electricity Authority (NEA) by utilities on the bordering Indian states of Bihar, Uttar Pradesh, and Uttarakhand. There are 12 cross-border bilateral power exchange facilities operating at 11 kV, 33 kV, and 132 kV levels, with tariffs decided by the Power Exchange Committee up to 50 MW. Additional purchases by Nepal beyond 50 MW are through licensed electricity traders under the India Electricity Market.

29   A 132 kV Tanakpur–Mahendranagar single circuit (S/C) line handles 70 MW power from Tanakpur HPP (120 MW) supplied by India to Nepal for free under the Mahakali Treaty. Nepal is now drawing around 400 MW power from India, and additional Nepal system strengthening was implemented to raise power imports from India to meet Nepal's domestic needs, as follows:

- 132 kV Katiya–Kusaha S/C on direct current DC line,
- 132 kV Raxaul–Parwanipur S/C on DC line, and
- 132 kV Muzaffarpur (India)–Dhalkebar (Nepal) line (designed to be upgraded to 400 kV).

30 The power trading Power Sale Agreement (PSA) was signed between NEA and PTC (Indian electricity trader) for the import of 150 MW for 25 years. A joint working group and joint study committee was formed by the governments of India and Nepal to deal with power trade and transmission connectivity between the two countries. The joint working group and joint study committee will draw up a long-term integrated transmission plan for evacuation of power from HPPs in Nepal, with detailed action plan to be prepared for HPPs coming up by 2025 (and a perspective plan for HPPs coming up by 2035).

(c) **India–Bangladesh**

31 A 400 kV alternating current (AC) Baharampur (India)–Bheramara (Bangladesh) line connected to HVDC back-to-back substations (commissioned in October 2013) enables India to export 500 MW of power to Bangladesh.[7] A second circuit with a similar arrangement of HVDC substations has been commissioned in September 2018, upgrading the power transmission capacity of the existing Bheramara interconnection between the two countries from 500 MW to 1,000 MW.[8] Implementation and system strengthening are undertaken for the Indian portion by Power Grid Corporation of India Limited (PGCIL) and for the Bangladesh portion by the Power Grid Company of Bangladesh Ltd.

32 A power purchase agreement was signed between Bangladesh Power Development Board (BPDB) and NTPC (India's largest power utility) for the supply of 250 MW from the unallocated share of Indian government in central generating stations, with pricing based on Central Electricity Regulatory Commission tariff. An agreement was signed between PTC and BPDB for Bangladesh's imports of 250 MW from the India market through competitive tendering process. In the second phase, BPDB has signed an agreement to import 300 MW from NTPC Vidyut Vyapar Nigam Limited. BPDB and PGCIL have entered into a transmission agreement for usage of interconnection facilities developed in India to export power to Bangladesh.

33 As per decision of the 8th Joint Steering Committee/Joint Working Group meeting, Bangladesh is at present importing up to 160 MW of power at Cumilla from Palatana in Tripura, India, through radial interconnection via the following cross-border links:

- Indian side: Surjyamaninagar (Tripura) to Bangladesh border 400 kV line (initially operated at 132 kV); and
- Bangladesh side: (i) Indian border–Cumilla (North) 400 kV DC line initially at 132 kV, and (ii) Cumilla (North) to Cumilla (South) 132 kV DC line.

34 A decision was made to enhance the capacity of the Cumilla interconnection to 500 MW at the 13th Joint Steering Committee/Joint Working Group meeting in 2017.

---

[7] ADB financed project in 2010 for a total project cost of $158.60 million (ADB financing of $100.00 million).

[8] ADB financed project in 2015 for a total project cost of $183.00 million (ADB financing of $120.00 million).

(d)   **India–Myanmar**

35   Myanmar's Ministry of Energy and Electricity has received proposals for importing power from India and the Lao People's Democratic Republic via cross-border transmission lines, which will support Myanmar's electrification program for border communities. Currently, India supplies power to Myanmar from Moreh (India) bordering Tamu (Myanmar) with a capacity of 3 MW at the unit price of ₹6.00/kilowatt-hour (kWh) (about $0.09/kWh).

36   **Prospects for Cross-Border Power Trade.** The SASEC Power Trade Working Group, during its inception meeting held in New Delhi, India, in October 2017, agreed on a list of potential SASEC generation and interconnection projects that would satisfy the SASEC OP's strategic objectives of (i) improving energy trade infrastructure; (ii) developing regional power markets in South Asia and (iii) developing low-carbon energy alternatives, and energy efficiency and conservation measures.[9] Key considerations in the selection should be (i) clean energy projects, (ii) strong export potential or future involving energy trade, and (iii) those which have yet to achieve financial closure.

37   The focus on cross-border interconnections is premised on the fact that hydropower and transmission investment requirements are huge, and if costs and benefits from these can be shared, then financial burdens can be reduced, cash flows smoothened, and project risks to individual countries lowered. Cross-border interconnections can also help balance the needs of national markets, given different demand and supply patterns of individual grids.

38   The focus on harnessing hydropower hinges on large viable potential available in Bhutan, India, and Nepal. By the end of 2017, Bhutan was able to harness 1,614 MW, which is only 7% of its viable capacity of 23,000 MW. Nepal has current installed capacity of only 803 MW, or only 2% of its viable potential of 43,000 MW. Of India's viable potential of 148,000 MW, only 45,000 MW has been harnessed, or 30% of the total.

HYDROPOWER GENERATION

39   Table 1 shows the potential hydropower generation projects, whose outputs are expected to be exported to one or more countries in SASEC (with or without consumption in the host country).

40   Kholongchhu and Chamkarchhu HPPs are joint venture projects to be carried out under the intergovernmental agreement signed by Bhutan and India back in 2014. Both will generate export revenues from power sales to India. Dorjilung and Nyera Amari HPPs, located in eastern Bhutan, will be developed by Bhutan's Druk Green Power Corporation or as agreed by the governments of Bangladesh, Bhutan, and India. Both will explore trilateral power arrangements, e.g., with power sale options to both Bangladesh and India.

----

[9]   ADB approved, in September 2018, regional technical assistance (RETA) to support SASEC regional energy cooperation with funding of $2.00 million. One of the technical assistance (TA) outputs is support for cross-border power trade through (i) workshops to promote effective trade arrangements and project assessments; and (ii) master plan development covering regional strategies, road maps, pre-feasibility studies, commercial/institutional arrangements, investment costs, regulations, and other focus areas. Another TA output is knowledge sharing on advanced energy technologies, which can include progress and issues of power trade experiences in other regions (Central Asia, Greater Mekong Subregion, etc.).

Table 1: Potential SASEC Hydropower Generation Projects

Country (Project site)	Relevant Possible Countries	Capacity (MW)	Commissioning Date	Project
1. BHU	BHU, IND	600	2022	Kholongchhu HPP
2. BHU	BHU, IND	770	2028	Chamkharchhu HPP
3. BHU	BAN, BHU, IND	1,125	2030	Dorjilung HPP
4. BHU	BHU, IND	404	2025	Nyera Amari HPP[a]
5. NEP	NEP, IND	900	2023	Arun 3 HPP
6. NEP	NEP, IND	840	Not available	Dudh Koshi HPP[b]
7. NEP	NEP, IND	410	2025–2026	Nalsing Gad HPP
8. NEP	NEP, IND, BAN	900	2022–2023	Upper Karnali HPP

BAN = Bangladesh, BHU = Bhutan, HPP = hydropower plant, IND = India, MW = megawatt, NEP = Nepal, SASEC = South Asia Subregional Economic Cooperation.

[a] Included in the Asian Development Bank's pipeline for Bhutan as SASEC Green Power Investment Program Tranches 1–3 in 2019, 2020, and 2021.

[b] Included in the Asian Development Bank's pipeline for Nepal in 2021 as Dudh Koshi Hydropower Project.

Source: Asian Development Bank.

41 Arun 3 and Dudh Koshi HPPs are in eastern Nepal and are among the most promising for export of power from Nepal to India; Arun 3 HPP will be developed by an Indian joint venture company and Dudh Koshi HPP by the NEA. Nalsing Gad HPP will be developed by a special purpose vehicle for speedy implementation. Upper Karnali HPP will be an export-oriented independent power producer, whose power is envisaged to be sold in Bangladesh and India.

(a)   **Potential Transmission Projects**

42 Table 2 shows the potential cross-border transmission lines that will make possible power trade between India–Bangladesh, India–Nepal, and India–Sri Lanka. As stated earlier, in the case of export HPPs in Bhutan, the associated transmission lines for power evacuation from the HPPs to the desired load centers are incorporated in the HPPs' engineering designs.

43 For the Tripura (India)–Cumilla (Bangladesh) line (item 1), a 400 kV line has been constructed to provide 160 MW to Bangladesh from the Palatana HPP in Tripura. Terminal equipment on the Bangladesh side needs to be upgraded to augment transmission capacity to 400 kV, and to install the 500 MW capacity HVDC back-to-back station in Cumilla to enable import of up to 500 MW from India. This 500 MW HVDC back-to-back station in Cumilla is under tendering being implemented by Power Grid Company of Bangladesh Ltd. with financing support from ADB and is expected to be completed by 2021.

44 For the Bihar (India)–Parbatipur (Bangladesh)–Assam (India) line (item 2), implementation will be in two phases. Phase 1 will involve connecting the three points via a 765 kV line for export of up to 500 MW into Bangladesh. Phase 2 will involve upgrading associated facilities to enable export of up to 1,000 MW into Bangladesh.

Table 2: Potential SASEC Cross-Border Transmission Projects

Countries	Name of Project
India–Bangladesh	1. Augmentation of transmission capacity from 132 kV to 400 kV between Surajmaninagar, Tripura, India–Cumilla, Bangladesh[a]
	2. Interconnection between Katihar, Bihar, India–Parbatipur, Bangladesh–Bornagar, Assam, India at 400 kV and augmentation to 765 kV
India–Nepal	3. Augmentation of transmission capacity between Dhalkebar, Nepal–Muzaffarpur, India from 132 kV to 400 kV
	4. 400 kV interconnection between Butwal, Nepal and Gorakhpur, India
India–Sri Lanka	5. Power interconnection detailed study

kV = kilovolt, SASEC = South Asia Subregional Economic Cooperation.

[a] Included in the Asian Development Bank's 2019 pipeline for Bangladesh as "SASEC Third Bangladesh–India Electrical Grid Interconnection Project."

Source: Asian Development Bank.

45   Currently, Dhalkerbar (Nepal) and Muzaffarpur (India) are connected at 400 kV, through which 145 MW is imported from India. The substation at Dhalkebar needs to be upgraded to 400 kV to increase transmission capacity from 132 kV to 400 kV. This will increase imports from India to 230 kV. The developers for both India and Bangladesh sides are the JV companies with both private sector and government entities (e.g., NEA and India's power grid enterprise, among others).

46   The 400 kV Butwal-Gorakhpur line is proposed as a backup to the Muzaffarpur–Dhalkebar line to ensure uninterrupted power supply, especially as surplus energy is produced from the Budhi Gandaki and Marshyangdi corridors when key HPPs are commissioned. However, initially, the line will be used to supply power to Nepal, especially Bhairahawa, Butwal, Pokhara, and Narayangadh.

47   A pre-feasibility study for the India–Sri Lanka interconnection was carried out with support from the United States Agency for International Development in 2002 and updated in 2006. In 2010, a memorandum of understanding was signed by India and Sri Lanka to conduct the feasibility study for the interconnection. The feasibility study was conducted by the Ceylon Electricity Board and PGCIL to recommend implementation of the 1,000 MW HVDC project, which will be carried out in two stages (1 x 500 MW monopole and 2 x 500 MW bipole). The 400 kV line segment will be built between Madurai and Anuradhapura, where HVDC converter stations will also be located. The proposed detailed study will recommend least-cost route alignment solutions.

48   Appendix 7 contains details on energy projects by country. Map 3 is the schematic map of hydropower plant locations and routes of key cross-border transmission lines.

Map 3: Existing and Proposed Cross-Border Power Trade Projects

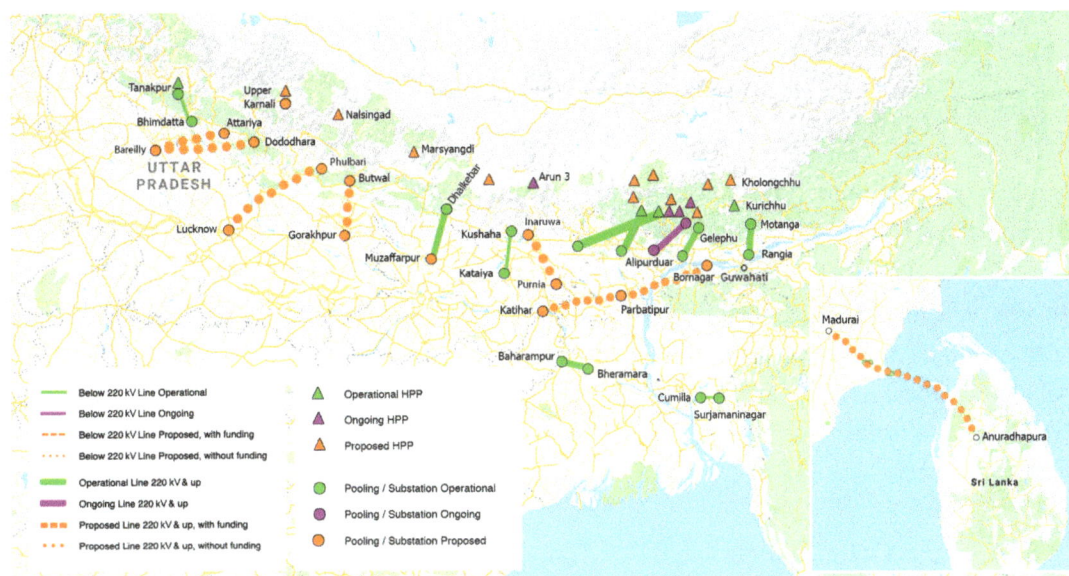

HPP = hydropower plant, kV = kilovolt.

Source: Asian Development Bank.

49   Status and Prospects of SASEC Oil and Gas Cooperation. Two of the identified flagship initiatives under the SASEC Vision involve trade in oil and gas, namely:[10] (i) pipeline corridor between Bangladesh and India for crude oil imports and product supply, and (ii) Sri Lanka as LPG transshipment and storage hub. The first is premised on Bangladesh's growing demand for imported refined petroleum products, while the northeast region of India has planned refinery capacity expansion way in excess of its requirements by 2025. The second is premised on Sri Lanka's strategic location, which may be leveraged to promote it as an LPG transshipment and logistics hub for the region. This can cater to not only for domestic demand but also supply to other countries in the SASEC subregion where LPG demand is fast growing.

(a)   **Bangladesh–India Oil and Gas Cooperation**

50   Bilateral discussions between Bangladesh and India have taken place regarding development of the SASEC Vision proposals for (i) the development of crude oil pipeline connectivity between Payra (Bangladesh) and refineries in Assam (India), and (ii) the development of petroleum product connectivity between the two countries. ADB missions to the two countries have looked into

---

[10]   One of the key outputs of the ADB-supported SASEC energy RETA approved in September 2018, is support for regional gas value chain, through (i) workshops covering capacity/knowledge support for market analysis, regulations, rules, gas safety management, among other things, without duplicating bilateral gas frameworks; and (ii) master plan development covering gas business strategies/road maps, commercial/institutional arrangements, development options, regulations, environmental impacts, and other focus areas. Another TA output is knowledge sharing on advanced energy technologies which can include operations of LNG/LPG terminals and storage facilities, and renewable energy and its battery substation facilities.

alternative proposals consistent with the overall bilateral hydrocarbon partnership framework, which include (i) assessment of LPG demand and opportunities for gas trade in Bangladesh; (ii) support for LPG market development in Bangladesh (bulk LPG imports, pipeline expansion to load centers); and (iii) regional energy planning studies in the context of Bangladesh's gas master plan and India's Hydrocarbon Vision 2030 for the northeast region.

51   **Bangladesh Gas Pipeline.** Both countries had entered into an agreement for the pipeline construction in April 2018. A 130-kilometer (km) pipeline will connect Siliguri in West Bengal in India and Parbatipur in Dinajpur district of Bangladesh. The project, which has an estimated cost of $47 million, will be completed in 30 months' time. The capacity of the pipeline will be 1 million metric tons per year. The pipeline project's 6 km section in India will be implemented by the Assam-based Numaligarh Refinery Limited, and the remaining 124 km of the pipeline project will be implemented by Bangladesh Petroleum Corporation. The project will replace the existing practice of sending diesel by railway covering 510 km.

(b)   **Sri Lanka as Liquefied Petroleum Gas Transshipment Hub**

52   Promoting Sri Lanka as an LPG hub hinges on its strategic location, and availability of port infrastructure and low-cost land space for storage. Having the LPG hub in Sri Lanka will reduce transport cost from the Middle East to South Asia and allow smaller vessels to serve fragmented regional markets (including Bangladesh, India, and Maldives). A stakeholders' workshop held in Colombo, Sri Lanka, in December 2017 confirmed the economic rationale for the hub, and agreed on the proposed scope of related studies, such as (i) needed regulatory reforms in Sri Lanka to enable private sector investment in the LPG hub, and (ii) development of small-scale LNG.

53   Setting up of the LPG hub in Sri Lanka could be undertaken without prejudice to the setting up of LPG hubs in other countries, subject to market demand. It was noted that development of LPG hubs is a private-led effort, and ADB support would be limited to creating an enabling environment through technical assistance and nonsovereign financing.

54   The agreed study on coordinated development of subregional infrastructure for LNG will focus on how small-scale LNG could meet potential subregional demand, linking with ongoing economic corridor studies. It will identify investment requirements to meet long-term emerging demand while exploring solutions to meet the short-term demand–supply gap with existing facilities. In the case of Maldives, a study would assess the viability of replacing diesel with LNG and small-scale LNG, through land-based or floating regasification units. Expected fuel cost reduction is in the range of 30%.

(c)   **Bilateral Cooperation in Oil and Gas Sector**

55   On a bilateral level, India is working on expanding cooperation with other SASEC member countries, particularly Myanmar and Nepal.

- **India–Nepal Cooperation in Oil and Gas Sector.** A joint working group on cooperation in the oil and gas sector has been formed to consider (i) construction of LPG pipeline from Motihari to Amlekhganj; (ii) construction of a natural gas pipeline from Gorakhpur to Sunwal;

and (iii) assistance of Indian Oil Corporation Limited for preparing a detailed project report (DPR) for extension of the petroleum products pipeline from Amlekhganj to Chitwan in Nepal. The 69 km pipeline from Motihari in Bihar to Amlekhganj in Nepal will deliver 2 million tons per year of petroleum products to the fuel-starved country and will be built at a cost of around $27.00 million. This will be South Asia's first transnational petroleum pipeline that will supply fuel to India's landlocked neighbor. Physical work of laying 13 km of the 69 km pipeline has been completed.

- **India–Myanmar Cooperation in Oil and Gas Sector.** The Hydrocarbon Vision 2030 for Northeast India envisages a natural gas pipeline from Numaligarh in Assam toward Sittwe in Myanmar in different phases. India is planning to set up an LNG import terminal in Myanmar. As part of bilateral cooperation in the oil sector, in September 2017, the first consignment of 30 metric tons of high-speed diesel was sent from India to Myanmar by land route. Numaligarh Refinery Limited dispatched the first diesel consignment through Moreh–Tamu border between the two countries. ADB is supporting the Government of India to develop the Imphal–Moreh road connectivity, which will further boost the supply of petroleum products along this route.

(d)   **SASEC Regional Gas and Petroleum Working Group**

56   The SASEC Regional Gas and Petroleum Working Group (RGP-WG) was established with the aim of enhancing the gas and fuel supply chain in the SASEC subregion; it is being supported by TA 9584-REG approved in September 2018. The RGP-WG's inception meeting, held in Delhi, India, in December 2018, agreed on its priority tasks which included (i) reviewing prospects for SASEC oil and gas cooperation with assessment of the cross-border supply and demand landscape; (ii) assessing each SASEC member's capacities to engage in hydrocarbon trade; (iii) sharing knowledge on technological advances in the oil and gas sector; (iv) looking into the enabling economic, regulatory, and institutional environment for the SASEC gas value chain; and (v) defining the RGP-WG's role, including its composition, focus areas, and work plan. The RGP-WG meeting in Delhi resulted in the following important outcomes:

- Identified regional projects/programs for physical construction and thematic studies for the working group's future monitoring and financing discussions (e.g., gas/petroleum pipelines, refinery expansion, LNG/LPG storage facility for break-bulk supply, LNG facility development);
- Inclusion of biofuel program as part of the regional agenda;
- Exchanged information/knowledge on gas/petroleum cooperation, other regions' approaches and practices, advance technological aspects, regulatory frameworks, and way forward programs; and
- Identified focal persons from each member country for subsequent working group activities.

V SUMMARY

A. TRANSPORT

57   The analysis of nearly completed and ongoing transport sector projects in the SASEC subregion shows substantial progress in terms of enhancing multimodal and cross-border connectivity following the alignment of defined SASEC road and railway corridors.

58   In road transport, a total of 58 projects costing $21.91 billion are being implemented, and some are near completion. Most of these are located along corridors 2 and 3, comprising a total of 40 projects costing $16.53 billion. Bangladesh and India comprise the bulk of nearly completed and/or ongoing projects, with 13 projects valued at $15.08 billion in Bangladesh, and 31 projects valued at $3.49 billion in India (Table 3).

Table 3: Nearly Completed or Ongoing Road Projects

Country	Projects (Number)	Cost ($ million)
Bangladesh	13	15,083.00
Bhutan	3	21.00
India	31	3,489.00
Myanmar	4	955.00
Nepal	4	720.00
Sri Lanka	3	1,645.00
Total	58	21,913.00
Road Corridor[a]		
SASEC Road Corridor 1	7	928.00
SASEC Road Corridor 2	16	13,567.00
SASEC Road Corridor 3	24	2,963.00
SASEC Road Corridor 4	9	3,120.00
SASEC Road Corridor 5	0	0.00
SASEC Road Corridor 6	3	1,645.00

SASEC = South Asia Subregional Economic Cooperation.

[a] Corridor totals do not add up as some projects are listed in two corridors.

Source: Asian Development Bank.

59   Progress has also been substantial in the other transport subsectors. There are 4 ongoing or nearly completed railway projects with total cost of $3.26 billion, 2 port projects costing $2.60 billion, and 10 airport projects costing almost $3.66 billion (Table 4).

Table 4: Nearly Completed or Ongoing Railway, Port, and Airport Projects

Country	Railway		Port		Airport	
	Number	Cost ($ million)	Number	Cost ($ million)	Number	Cost ($ million)
Bangladesh	3	3,215.00	2	2,601.00	3	1,849.00
Bhutan					1	2.00
India	1	50.00			2	521.00
Myanmar					2	671.00
Nepal					1	65.00
Sri Lanka					1	550.00
Total	4	3,265.00	2	2,601.00	10	3,658.00

Source: Asian Development Bank.

60   Nevertheless, there remain huge requirements to fully realize the envisioned transport connectivity along the identified SASEC road corridors. There are 35 projects costing $18.30 billion that have identified financing, although some have no committed financing yet (as indicated in the status column of the Appendix tables). A fewer number (12 projects costing $3.63 billion) do not have identified financing yet and have lower levels of project preparedness (Table 5).

Table 5: Proposed and Potential SASEC Road Projects

Country	Projects with Identified Financing[a]		Projects without Identified Financing	
	Number	Cost ($ million)	Number	Cost ($ million)
Bangladesh	10	11,425	6	3,247
Bhutan	0	0	1	20
India	10	1,119	4	322
Myanmar	5	560	1	42
Nepal	6	2,152	0	0
Sri Lanka	4	3,040	0	0
Total	35	18,296	12	3,631
Road Corridor[b]				
SASEC Road Corridor 1	3	1,677	2	272
SASEC Road Corridor 2	7	5,788	3	200
SASEC Road Corridor 3	12	1,305	2	62
SASEC Road Corridor 4	10	6,472	3	1,498
SASEC Road Corridor 5	2	621	2	1,599
SASEC Road Corridor 6	4	3,040	0	0

SASEC = South Asia Subregional Economic Cooperation.

[a] With identified financing, which may or may not have financing commitment.

[b] Corridor totals differ from country totals because some projects are listed in more than one corridor.

Source: Asian Development Bank.

61   The combined financing requirements for proposed railway, port, and airport projects are also large but lower than those for roads (Table 6). For railway, financing needed by projects without identified financier ($266.70 million) is far less than the cost of projects with identified financier ($4.82 billion), which is mainly because the cost of six out of eight proposed railway projects in Bangladesh has yet to be finalized. For ports, the cost is also larger for projects with identified financing ($8.82 billion versus $1.03 billion). Airport development also has large financing needs—$2.09 billion for three projects with identified financing source, more than those with no identified financing ($200.00 million for one project).

Table 6: Proposed Railway, Port, and Airport Projects

| | Proposed Projects with Identified Financing | | | | | |
| | Railway | | Port | | Airport | |
Country	Number	Cost ($ million)	Number	Cost ($ million)	Number	Cost ($ million)
Bangladesh	6	4,815.00	4	5,186.83		
Bhutan					1	55.00
India			4	3,437.00		
Myanmar					1	1,812.00
Nepal					1	220.00
Sri Lanka			1	200.00		
Total	**6**	**4,815.00**	**9**	**8,823.83**	**3**	**2,087.00**
	Proposed Projects without Identified Financing					
Bangladesh	8[a]	266.70				
Bhutan					1	200.00
Sri Lanka			2	1,030.00		
Total	**8**	**266.70**	**2**	**1,030.00**	**1**	**200.00**

[a] Bangladesh Railways noted that costing of six out of eight projects has yet to be finalized.

Source: Asian Development Bank.

B. TRADE FACILITATION

62   The trade facilitation pipeline consists of 16 projects with total cost of $425.86 million (Table 7). The largest requirements are by Bangladesh (four projects costing $299.00 million) followed by India (six projects costing $72.00 million). More than half of the projects are infrastructure related: (i) eight projects costing $329.00 million on trade-related infrastructure, and (ii) one project costing approximately $17.00 million on sanitary and phytosanitary–technical barriers to trade-related infrastructure. The remaining seven projects costing $79.90 million will support technical assistance for (i) enhancing trade documentation processes ($53.50 million), and (ii) automation in border agencies and development of NSWs ($26.40 million).

Table 7: Trade Facilitation Priority Projects and Country Breakdown

Sector/ Area	BAN	BHU	IND	MLD	MYA	NEP	Total
	($ million)						Total
a. Simplify trade documentation, increase automation, and expedite border clearance and capacity building	49.00 (2)		2.00 (1)		0.50 (1)	2.00 (1)	53.50 (5)
b. Promote automation in border agencies and facilitate the development of national single windows		14.40 (1)		12.00 (1)			26.40 (2)
c. SPS–TBT-related infrastructure development and MRA				16.96 (1)			16.96 (1)
d. Development of trade-related infrastructure in land ports, ICDs	250.00 (2)		70.00 (5)			9.00 (1)	329.00 (8)
Total Trade Facilitation	**299.00 (4)**	**14.40 (1)**	**72.00 (6)**	**28.96 (2)**	**0.50 (1)**	**11.00 (2)**	**425.86 (16)**

BAN = Bangladesh, BHU = Bhutan, ICD = inland container depot, IND = India, MLD = Maldives, MRA = mutual recognition arrangements, MYA = Myanmar, NEP = Nepal, SPS = sanitary and phytosanitary, TBT = technical barriers to trade.

Note: Numbers in parentheses indicate the number of projects.

Source: Asian Development Bank.

C. ENERGY

63 The financing requirements for energy projects are large. Already, completed and/or ongoing projects are taking up over $5.44 billion in funding. Expansion of hydropower generation capacity for power export purposes in the next few years will further elevate the needed financing for energy projects. Twelve projects with required financing of $11.42 billion have identified financing sources and 8 projects costing about $7.90 billion do not have identified financing yet (Table 8). By energy subsector, hydropower takes up the bulk of financing required, reaching $17.88 billion for 12 proposed projects in Bhutan and Nepal. Cross-border power interconnections to enable power trade take up about $1.14 billion for six proposed projects. So far, only two proposed oil and gas projects take up $302.40 million, but this subsector is expected to pick up as more progress is achieved and additional requirements identified in developing the SASEC Vision flagship program in oil and gas.

Table 8: Energy Projects and Country Breakdown, by Status

Country	Completed or Ongoing Projects		Proposed Projects (with identified financing)		Proposed Projects (without identified financing)	
	Number	Cost ($ million)	Number	Cost ($ million)	Number	Cost ($ million)
Bangladesh	4	610.00	1	202.40	1	TBD
Bhutan	4	3,491.00	5	7,200.00	3	7,100.00
Nepal	2	1,341.00	6	4,015.20	2	150.00
Sri Lanka					2	654.00
Total	**10**	**5,442.00**	**12**	**11,417.60**	**8**	**7,904.00**

TBD = to be determined.

Source: Asian Development Bank.

Table 9: Proposed Energy Projects and Country Breakdown, by Energy Subsector
(with and without identified financing, $ million)

| Country | Hydropower Generation | | Cross-Border Transmission | | Oil and Gas | |
	Number	Cost ($ million)	Number	Cost ($ million)	Number	Cost ($ million)
Bangladesh			1	TBD	1	202.40
Bhutan	8	14,300.00				
Nepal	4	3,577.00	4	588.20		
Sri Lanka			1	554.00	1	100.00
Total	**12**	**17,877.00**	**6**	**1,142.20**	**2**	**302.40**

TBD = to be determined.

Source: Asian Development Bank.

D. SUMMARY

64 Overall, the SASEC OP consists of 112 proposed projects with financing requirement of about $58.90 billion (Table 10). The bulk of proposed projects are in the transport sector, with 76 projects requiring $39.15 billion. Country-wise, Bangladesh has the largest funding requirement of $25.44 billion for 40 projects mostly in transport, followed by Bhutan ($14.59 billion), which involves mostly hydropower development. India's and Sri Lanka's funding requirements for transport and energy are also large: at $4.95 billion (India) and $4.92 billion (Sri Lanka).

Table 10: SASEC Operational Plan Proposed SASEC Projects, by Sector
(both with and without identified financing)

| Sector/Subsector | Cost ($ million) and Number[a] | | | | | | |
	Bangladesh	Bhutan	India	Maldives	Myanmar	Nepal	Sri Lanka
Roads	14,672.00 (16)	20.00 (1)	1,441.00 (14)		602.00 (6)	2,152.00 (6)	3,040.00 (4)
Railway	5,081.70 (14)						
Ports	5,186.83 (4)		3,437.00 (4)				1,230.00 (3)
Airports		255.00 (2)			1,812.00 (1)	220.00 (1)	
Total Transport	24,940.53 (34)	275.00 (3)	4,878.00 (18)		2,414.00 (7)	2,372.00 (7)	4,270.00 (7)
Total Trade Facilitation	299.00 (4)	14.40 (1)	72.00 (6)	28.96 (2)	0.50 (1)	11.00 (2)	

continued next page

Table 10: *Continued*

Sector/Subsector	Cost ($ million) and Number[a]						
	Bangladesh	Bhutan	India	Maldives	Myanmar	Nepal	Sri Lanka
Hydropower		14,300.00 (8)				3,577.00 (4)	
Cross-Border Transmission	TBD (1)					588.20 (4)	554.00 (1)
Oil and Gas	202.40 (1)						100.00 (1)
Total Energy	202.40 (2)	14,300.00 (8)				4,165.20 (8)	654.00 (2)
GRAND TOTAL[b]	25,441.93 (40)	14,589.40 (12)	4,950.00 (24)	28.96 (2)	2,414.50 (8)	6,548.20 (17)	4,924.00 (9)

SASEC = South Asia Subregional Economic Cooperation, TBD = to be determined.

[a] Numbers in parentheses indicate the number of projects.

[b] The grand total of all proposed projects (with and without identified financing) is $58.90 billion for 112 projects.

Source: Asian Development Bank.

65 However, if we go by more prepared projects with identified financing (but not necessarily with funding commitment), the SASEC OP pipeline is reduced considerably to 78 projects with financing requirement of about $45.84 billion (Table 11). Transport still takes up the bulk of financing required, at $34.02 billion for 53 projects. Bangladesh still has the largest portfolio of projects with identified financing, at $21.93 billion for 25 projects, followed by Bhutan ($7.27 billion for seven projects) and Nepal ($6.39 billion for 13 projects).

Table 11: **SASEC Operational Plan Proposed SASEC Projects, by Sector (with identified financing)**

Sector/Subsector	Cost ($ million) and Number[a]						
	Bangladesh	Bhutan	India	Maldives	Myanmar	Nepal	Sri Lanka
Roads	11,425.00 (10)		1,119.00 (10)		560.00 (5)	2,152.00 (6)	3,040.00 (4)
Railway	4,815.00 (6)						
Ports	5,186.83 (4)		3,437.00 (4)				200.00 (1)
Airports		55.00 (1)			1,812.00 (1)	220.00 (1)	
Total Transport	21,426.83 (20)	55.00 (1)	4,556.00 (14)		2,372.00 (6)	2,372.00 (7)	3,240.00 (5)
Total Trade Facilitation	299.00 (4)	14.40 (1)	72.00 (4)	28.96 (2)	0.50 (1)		

continued next page

Table 11: *Continued*

Sector/Subsector	Cost ($ million) and Number[a]						
	Bangladesh	Bhutan	India	Maldives	Myanmar	Nepal	Sri Lanka
Hydropower		7,200.00 (5)				3,427.00 (3)	
Cross-Border Transmission						588.20 (3)	
Oil and Gas	202.40 (1)						
Total Energy	202.40 (1)	6,800.00 (5)				4,015.20 (5)	
Grand Total[b]	21,928.23 (25)	7,269.40 (7)	4,628.00 (20)	12.00 (1)	2,372.50 (7)	6,387.20 (13)	3,240.00 (5)

SASEC = South Asia Subregional Economic Cooperation, TBD = to be determined.

[a] Numbers in parentheses indicate the number of projects.

[b] The grand total of projects with identified financing is $45.84 billion for 78 projects.

Source: Asian Development Bank.

APPENDIX 1

SASEC ROAD CORRIDORS FOR THE SASEC OPERATIONAL PLAN

SASEC Road Corridor 1: "Nepal–Kolkata Trade Corridor": Kathmandu–Birgunj–Raxaul–Muzaffarpur–Patna–Gaya–Asansol–Kolkata–Haldia (1,023 km), including 1a: future route Kathmandu–Birgunj (125 km); and 1b: link roads to Haldia Port (127 km)

SASEC Road Corridor 1 is the key trade route linking landlocked Nepal with its largest trading partner, India, as well as for trade with third countries passing through Kolkata Port or Haldia Port. On the Nepalese section, the challenging terrain will inhibit upgrading roads to Asian Highway (AH) Classification Class II or higher, except for areas north of the Terai Plains, and for the areas to be traversed by the "Fast Track Road" (Kathmandu to Nijgadh) in the southern Terai region. From Pathlaiya south to the border at Birgunj, 4-laning is possible and needed, as both traffic and economic activities along this road are leading to congestion. This section includes a new link road between the Birgunj bypass and the new Integrated Border Post provided by India. On the Indian side of the border, there have been some delays on the upgrading of the Raxaul–Motihari road section, especially the link road into the new border facility. The NH28 remains a single carriageway southward to Pipra Kothi, south of Motihari, and widening of the road has been delayed by contractual problems. Contracts are due to be terminated and re-awarded, though the short-distance link between Motihari and the start of the dual carriageway at Pipra Kothi is not identified as part of this recontracting process. The section from Pipra Kothi all the way to Kolkata is intended to be Asian Highway Class 1 dual carriageway, though between Muzaffarpur and the junction with the NH2 Delhi–Kolkata highway at Dobhi, this dualling appears incomplete in some sections. As the road approaches Kolkata, traffic increases significantly, which is the main reason for the proposal to provide extra lanes between Panagarth and Dankuni on the outskirts of the city.

Table A1.1: SASEC Road Corridor 1

Project No.	Project Name	Estimated Cost ($ million)	Status
NEP-RD-01	Upgrading of Kathmandu: Naubise–Mugling road	257.00	Project planned and funding identified, which may or may not be finalized
NEP-RD 02	Upgrading of Mugling–Narayanghat highway	310.00	Project completed or under implementation
NEP-RD-03	Upgrading of Pathlaiya–Hetauda–Narayanghat road	220.00	Project planned and funding identified, which may or may not be finalized
NEP-RD-04	Construction of a new 4-lane expressway from Kathmandu to Nijgadh	1,200.00	Project planned and funding identified, which may or may not be finalized
NEP-RD-05	Upgrading of Pathlaiya–Birgunj road	30.00	Project completed or under implementation
IND-RD-01	Upgrading of Raxaul–Motihari road section	100.00	Project completed or under implementation

continued next page

Table A1.1: *Continued*

Project No.	Project Name	Estimated Cost ($ million)	Status
IND-RD-02	Upgrading of Motihari–Pipra Kothi road section	22.00	Project planned but no funding identified
IND-RD–C01	Pipra Kothi–Muzaffarpur road	NA	Project completed or under implementation
IND-RD-03	Upgrading of Muzaffarpur–Patna road section	95.00	Project completed or under implementation
IND-RD-04	Expansion of Patna–Gaya road section	160.00	Project completed or under implementation
IND-RD-05	Widening of Gaya–Dobhi road	38.00	Project completed or under implementation
IND-RD–C02	Dobhi–Panagarth	NA	Project completed or under implementation
IND-RD-06	Widening of Panagarth–Dankuni road section	195.00	Project completed or under implementation
IND-RD-07	Development of Road Connections to Diamond Harbor	250.00	Project planned but no funding identified

NA = not available, SASEC = South Asia Subregional Economic Cooperation.

Sources: Country submissions; ADB consultant's report.

Transit for international trade (using Kolkata Port) travels via various routes in the city—all of which are congested with urban traffic. This establishes the need for a freight curfew that limits transits to evening and night movements. There have been proposals to construct a new container port at Diamond Harbor on the east bank of the Hooghly River, which would require a new upgraded route. Since the proposal for the port appears to have been suspended, these upgrades may not be necessary. Conversely, transits using Haldia Port bypass Kolkata city and can use dual carriageway all the way to the port.

SASEC Road Corridor 2: "Bay of Bengal Highway": Thoothukudi–Chennai–Visakhapatnam–Kolkata–Benapole–Jessore–Narail–New Padma Bridge–Dhaka–Chattogram (formerly Chittagong)–Cox's Bazar (2,921 km), including 2a: Akhaura–Agartala spur (10 km) and 2b: Bariarhat–Ramgarh spur (50 km)

SASEC Corridor 2 consists initially of the important Indian Eastern Coast Corridor that links all the Indian SASEC ports. The proposed ring road around Maduai has no confirmed funding allowing implementation, but the rest of the southern section Thoothukudi–Chennai is already dual carriageway. There are problems with accessibility to Chennai Port, where the elevated access road has been stalled for some years. The main section of the Chennai–Kolkata link that forms part of the "Golden Quadrilateral" is already dual carriageway, but due to the high levels of traffic, it needs to be widened to 6 lanes at the southern and northern ends. The roads around the north of Kolkata are highly congested and remedial solutions include elevated roadways. The road north is shown as NH35 but has, in the past, been disputed as a state road as it leaves Kolkata. It is not only the main road to the northeastern states but is also the key trade route for land-based bilateral trade between India

Table A1.2: SASEC Road Corridor 2

Project No.	Project Name	Estimated Cost ($ million)	Status
IND-RD-C03	Thoothukudi–Madurai Road	NA	Project completed or under implementation
IND-RD-08	Upgrading of Madurai Ring Road	30.00	Project planned but no funding identified
IND-RD-C04	Madurai–Chennai Road	NA	Project completed or under implementation
IND-RD-09	Construction of Elevated Expressway to Chennai Port	225.00	Project completed or under implementation
IND-RD-10	Expansion of Chennai–Tada road section	60.00	Project completed or under implementation
IND-RD-11	Expansion of Tada–Nellore road section	73.00	Project planned and funding identified, which may or may not be finalized
IND-RD-C05	Nellore–Bhubaneshwar	NA	Project completed or under implementation
IND-RD-12	Widening of Bhubaneshwar–Chandikhole road section	150.00	Project completed or under implementation
IND-RD-13	Upgrading of Chandikhole road–Paradeep port	115.00	Project planned and funding identified, which may or may not be finalized
IND-RD-14	Expansion of Chandikhole–Bhadrak road	210.00	Project completed or under implementation
IND-RD-15	Improvement of Bhadrak–Belasore road	34.00	Project completed or under implementation
IND-RD-16	Improvement of Belasore–Kharagpur road	67.00	Project completed or under implementation
IND-RD-C06	Kharagpur–Dankuni	NA	Project completed or under implementation
IND-RD-17	Upgrading of the Belgharia Expressway	20.00	Project planned but no funding identified
IND-RD-18	Improvement of Barasat–Bangaon road connecting Kolkata to Bangladesh border	130.00	Project planned and funding identified, which may or may not be finalized
BAN-RD-01	Benapole–Jessore road	41.00	Project completed or under implementation
BAN-RD-02	New alignment of AH1 Bhanga–Narail–Jessore–Benapole road	920.00	Project planned and funding identified, which may or may not be finalized
BAN-RD-03	New Padma Bridge	2,900.00	Project completed or under implementation
BAN-RD-04	New Padma Bridge approach roads	1,000.00	Project completed or under implementation
BAN-RD-05	Northern link road	860.00	Project completed or under implementation

continued next page

Table A1.2: *Continued*

Project No.	Project Name	Estimated Cost ($ million)	Status
BAN-RD-06	Construction of the Dhaka Elevated Expressway	1,132.00	Project completed or under implementation
BAN-RD-07	Construction of the Dhaka–Ashulia Elevated Expressway	2,098.00	Project completed or under implementation
BAN-RD-08	Construction of the Dhaka East–West Elevated Expressway	2,049.00	Project completed or under implementation
BAN-RD-C01	Dhaka–Chattogram Road	NA	Project completed or under implementation
BAN-RD-09	Kanchpur, Meghna, and Gumpti bridges	1,061.00	Project completed or under implementation
BAN-RD-29	Development of Ashunganj–Akhaura–Agartala road	430.00	Project completed or under implementation
BAN-RD-10	Rehabilitation of Baraierhat–Heako–Ramgarh roads	100.00	Project planned and funding identified, which may or may not be finalized
BAN-RD-11	Chattogram Port Access Road Improvement	150.00	Project planned but no funding identified
BAN-RD-12	Construction of new Dhaka–Chattogram Expressway on PPP basis	2,750.00	Project planned and funding identified, which may or may not be finalized
BAN-RD-13	Karnaphuli Multi-Channel Tunnel Project	1,250.00	Project completed or under implementation
BAN-RD-14	Improvement of Chattogram–Cox's Bazar Highway through PPP	1,700.00	Project planned and funding identified, which may or may not be finalized

NA = not available, PPP = public–private partnership, SASEC = South Asia Subregional Economic Cooperation.
Sources: Asian Development Bank; country submissions in 2018.

and Bangladesh via the Petrapole–Benapole crossing. Presently, trucks route farther north to reach the border crossing using a rehabilitated state (as the direct road to the border is heavily congested and has curfews). A new alignment of NH35 is required to avoid the many villages on the way to the border. The actual border crossing is very congested, and trucks take several days from Kolkata to discharge their cargo at Benapole, as no through freight transport is permitted. It is hoped, under a bilateral agreement, that increased volumes of through-transport may be allowed. The current road alignment is via the N7 and a ferry crossing, but a new multipurpose bridge is being constructed further downstream and a new 4-lane, 137 km highway is required from Jessore to the bridge. On the western bank, the new highway from Mawa to Dhaka is well advanced. The main road from Dhaka to Chattogram is now all 4-laned but is still very busy: aside from handling a sizable 30% share of Bangladesh's international trade, it also handles domestic traffic between the country's largest cities. Due to this condition, there are proposals for the construction of a supplementary Public–Private Partnership Expressway. Improvements to port accessibility at Chattogram have already been undertaken, but, further out, there is a need to expand the approach roads to 6 lanes. Upgrading the route south of Chattogram has already commenced with the construction of a tunnel under the

Karnaphuli River. The route south through to Cox's Bazar has much lower levels of traffic. This route could help promote Cox's Bazar as a tourist destination and could also form part of a possible future extension to Myanmar. The corridor development strategy is to upgrade all of the corridors to Asian Highway (AH) Class 1–dual carriageway. The two spur roads, namely, (i) Akhaura–Agartala spur (10 km), and (ii) Bariarhat–Ramgarh spur (50 km), are to be developed to connect the northeastern states of India with Chattogram Port in Bangladesh.

SASEC Road Corridor 3: "India–ASEAN East–West Corridor": Kolkata–Siliguri–Guwahati–Dimapur–Imphal–Moreh/Tamu–Mandalay–Bago–Myawaddy (3,039 km), including spur roads 3a: Hasimara–Phuentsholing–Thimphu (192 km); and 3b: Bago–Yangon (68 km)

SASEC Corridor 3 is the key route for landlocked Bhutan, enabling it to use the Indian ports for third country trade and includes the important "Chicken's Neck" Siliguri Corridor as the route likely to be used for land-based trade between India and Myanmar. The first road section northward from Kolkata is the same State Road as Corridor 2 until the turning eastward to Petrapole. The sections north of Khrishnagar toward Siliguri are all being 4-laned but have been subject to long delays. Progress in 4-laning is particularly slow and likely to take many more years before completion. There are long delays at Dalkhola, until the bypass is completed. Traffic levels are high, predominantly with domestic traffic and some Bhutanese movements. The next section between Siliguri and Guwahati is more advanced in terms of completed 4-laning than the previous section. This section is also heavily trafficked, mainly by domestic transport. The traffic for Bhutan diverts northward at Hasimara toward the Bhutanese border at Phuentsholing. This 2-lane road is being upgraded with Asian Development Bank (ADB) funding as part of the project to improve the roads connecting Bhutan and Bangladesh. A new border facility is being constructed at Pasakha and, therefore, a connecting road is required. The Thimphu–Phuentsholing Highway has been completed and is mainly AH Class III. The next section of the main corridor is from Guwahati to Nagoan and as far as Dabaka it is now all dual carriageway. The next section for Dabaka to Dimapur passes through the edge of the Rengma Hills, and some sections are likely to remain AH Class II. Traffic levels on this section are lower and are dominated by domestic traffic destined for northeastern states. Similarly, the next sections from Dimapur to Kohima and Imphal are being gradually upgraded to AH Class II, and 4-laning is likely to be limited as most of the route is through hilly or mountainous terrain. From Imphal to the Myanmar border at Moreh–Tamu, the route is to be upgraded with ADB assistance. Trade through the border consists predominantly of localized cross-border trade and goods coming through from the People's Republic of China (PRC), mainly hardware and plastic goods. Since through-transport of freight vehicles is not permitted, trucks must transship their loads at the border. Current volumes are low, partly because of the poor quality of the roads on either side of the border which are being gradually improved, and partly due to the low population in the regions on either side of the border. As these roads are improved and transit times are reduced, it is anticipated that trade will increase. On the Myanmar side, the road southward from Tamu to Kalewa has been upgraded by the Government of India, though some bridge works remain. Traffic levels are relatively low, and monsoon conditions can make this journey difficult. The next section from Kalewa to Yargi is particularly demanding in the monsoon season, as it crosses several mountain ranges. Work on this section will be undertaken by the Government of India and is scheduled to commence soon. From Yargi south and east through Monywa and on to Mandalay, the road has been upgraded to AH Class II. The road from Mandalay to Yangon via Bago is heavily trafficked by freight vehicles that are unable to use the expressway.

Traffic volumes are high and mainly relate to domestic north–south movements, though there is also significant trade with the PRC coming through the Muse border post. The AH1 north of Bago meets the NH8 and continues to Yangon. This section is already 4-laned and is in good condition. There are plans to connect the NH8 with the Thilawa port that lies to the south. The absence of this connection has delayed the transition of much of the container traffic from central Yangon to Thilawa. Near Bago, the corridor travels east and southward along the coast toward Thaton. This section of road has been upgraded and has reasonable traffic levels of both domestic traffic to and from the south and trade movements from Thailand. From Thaton, the road travels inland through the mountains to the Thai border. This road is gradually being upgraded to AH Class II with funding by the Government of Thailand and ADB. Because this road passes through hilly terrain and has several major river crossings, the project completion date has been extended.

Table A1.3: SASEC Road Corridor 3

Project No.	Project Name	Estimated Cost ($ million)	Status
IND-RD-18	Improvement of Barasat–Bangaon road connecting Kolkata to Bangladesh border	130.00	Project planned and funding identified, which may or may not be finalized
IND-RD-19	Upgrading of Barasat–Krishnanagar road section	124.00	Project completed or under implementation
IND-RD-20	Upgrading of Krishnanagar–Berhampore road	107.00	Project completed or under implementation
IND-RD-21	Upgrading of Berhampore–Farakka road section	150.00	Project completed or under implementation
IND-RD-22	Upgrading of Farakka–Raiganj road section	154.00	Project completed or under implementation
IND-RD-23	Upgrading of Raiganj–Dalkhola road section	83.00	Project completed or under implementation
IND-RD-C07	4-laning of Dalkhola–Ghoshpukur	NA	Project completed or under implementation
IND-RD-24	Expansion of Ghoshpukur–Siliguri road section	31.00	Project completed or under implementation
IND-RD-25	Upgrading of Ghoshpukur–Bipara section	200.00	Project planned and funding identified, which may or may not be finalized
IND-RD-26	Upgrading of Bipara–Salsalabari road section	105.00	Project planned and funding identified, which may or may not be finalized
IND-RD-45	Upgrading of Hasimara–Jaigaon road section	25.00	Project completed or under implementation
IND-RD-41	Construction of link road to Pasakha ICD	10.00	Project completed or under implementation
IND-RD-27	Upgrading of Salsalabari–Bijni section of NH31C	150.00	Project completed or under implementation

continued next page

Table A1.3: *Continued*

Project No.	Project Name	Estimated Cost ($ million)	Status
IND-RD-28	Upgrading of Bijni–Baihata section NH31C	600.00	Project completed or under implementation
IND-RD-29	Upgrading of Baihata–Guwahati section of NH31C	45.00	Project completed or under implementation
IND-RD-C08	4-laning of Guwahati–Nagoan road	NA	Project completed or under implementation
IND-RD-C09	4-laning of Nagoan–Dabaka road	NA	Project completed or under implementation
IND-RD-30	Upgrading of Dabaka–Dimapur road to passes through the edge of the Rengma Hills 2–4 lanes	165.00	Project completed or under implementation
IND-RD-31	Upgrading of Dimapur–Kohima	55.00	Project completed or under implementation
IND-RD-32	Upgrading of Dimapur–Kohima	49.00	Project completed or under implementation
IND-RD-33	Upgrading of Dimapur–Kohima	49.00	Project completed or under implementation
IND-RD-34	Assam–Nagaland connectivity 1	55.00	Project completed or under implementation
IND-RD-35	Assam–Nagaland connectivity 2	56.00	Project planned and funding identified, which may or may not be finalized
IND-RD-36	Improvement to Kohima–Mao road section	64.00	Project planned and funding identified, which may or may not be finalized
IND-RD-37	Improvement to Mao–Imphal road section	189.00	Project planned and funding identified, which may or may not be finalized
IND-RD-38	Improvement of Imphal–Moreh road	135.00	Project completed or under implementation
IND-RD-39	Construction of Moreh Bypass	1.00	Project planned and funding identified, which may or may not be finalized
BHU-RD-01	Construction of Phuentsholing–Chamkuna Road	7.00	Project completed or under implementation
BHU-RD-02	Construction of Pasakha Access Road (PAR)	7.00	Project completed or under implementation
BHU-RD-03	Construction of Northern Bypass Road	7.00	Project completed or under implementation
BHU-RD-04	Improvement of Rinchending (Kharbandi) to Jumja Road	20.00	Project planned but no funding identified
MYA-RD-01	Rehabilitation of Tamu–Kyigone–Kalewa (TKK) Road	143.00	Project completed or under implementation
MYA-RD-02	Construction of Kalewa–Yargi Road	190.00	Project completed or under implementation

continued next page

Table A1.3: *Continued*

Project No.	Project Name	Estimated Cost ($ million)	Status
MYA-RD-C01	Yargi–Monywa	NA	Project completed or under implementation
MYA-RD-C02	Monywa–Mandalay	NA	Project completed or under implementation
MYA-RD-03	Upgrading of Mandalay–Bago road	500.00	Project completed or under implementation
MYA-RD-C03	4-laning of Upgrading of Bago–Yangon road	NA	Project completed or under implementation
MYA-RD-04	Safety improvement on Yangon–Mandalay Expressway	91.00	Project planned and funding identified, which may or may not be finalized
MYA-RD-05	Construction of new bridge across Bago River	289.00	Project planned and funding identified, which may or may not be finalized
MYA-RD-06	Bago Bypass Project	25.00	Project planned and funding identified, which may or may not be finalized
MYA-RD-07	Upgrade of Bago–Thilawa road	104.00	Project planned and funding identified, which may or may not be finalized
MYA-RD-08	Thilawa–East Dagon Road Project	42.00	Project planned but no funding identified
MYA-RD-C04	Upgrading of Bago–Thaton Road	NA	Project completed or under implementation
MYA-RD-09	Upgrading of Thaton–Eindu Road	51.00	Project planned and funding identified, which may or may not be finalized
MYA-RD-10	Upgrading of Eindu–Kawkareik section	122.00	Project completed or under implementation
MYA-RD-C05	Upgrading of Kawkareik–Myawaddy road section	NA	Project completed or under implementation

NA = not available, BHU = Bhutan, IND = India, MYA = Myanmar, RD = road, SASEC = South Asia Subregional Economic Cooperation.
Sources: Asian Development Bank; country submissions in 2018.

SASEC Road Corridor 4: "Nepal–Bhutan–Bangladesh North–South Corridor": Kathmandu–Kakarvitta/Panitanki–Fulbari/Banglabandha–Rangpur–Hatikumrul–Dhaka–Chattogram (1,442 km), including spur roads 4a: Rangpur–Burimari/Changrabandha–Phuentsholing (291 km); 4b: Bogra–Jessore–Khulna–Mongla (331 km); and 4c: link roads to Payra Port (236 km)

SASEC Corridor 4 is important in the north for both landlocked Bhutan and Nepal, for their trade with Bangladesh and possible use of the Bangladesh ports. Trade and traffic volumes are initially relatively low and seasonal, but as the corridor continues southward, the overall volumes increase rapidly with substantial flow of domestic traffic and trade traffic traveling to and from the capital and the ports.

The initial section from Kathmandu to the junction with the east–west highway at Pathlaiya are the same as for Corridor 1. Traffic moving along the east–west highway is relatively light and consists mainly of domestic traffic, as most trade with India passes through the Birgunj border crossing. Volumes moving through the Kakarvitta border along the corridor across India to the Banglabandha border in Bangladesh are limited at this stage. Most of the traffic passing through these border posts is cross-border trade, much of it with Siliguri, which is an important trade center on Corridor 3. The traffic on Corridor 4a from Phuentsholing in Bhutan to the Burimari–Changrabandha crossing is small compared to trade with India using the initial Phuentsholing–Hasimara section. Both these links across the "Chicken's Neck" are being upgraded under SASEC programs. Through traffic between Bangladesh and Nepal, and between Bangladesh and Bhutan, can be particularly seasonal with fruit and vegetable movements. The links from both these borders south to Rangpur are scheduled to be upgraded, but programming and funding have yet to be finalized and contracts let. It is anticipated that ADB will provide funding for both these sections. Volumes of traffic are relatively light but increase significantly south of Rangpur. The sections from Rangpur southeastward to Dhaka are all under various stages of construction under the ADB SASEC program. While some sections are almost complete, especially toward Dhaka, it is anticipated that completion of the longer northerly section will take some years. The Corridor 4b spur road splits off the main corridor at Bogra. On the initial section Bogra–Natore, which has not been identified for development, volumes are significantly lower than volumes on the main corridor and are dominated by domestic traffic. The link between Natore–Jessore–Khulna–Mongla has been subject to preparatory studies under the SASEC program, but no firm funding proposal for implementing upgrades has been agreed at this stage. Traffic being routed through Mongla Port remains limited as few container lines provide regular calls at the port. The link between Dhaka and the proposed new deep-sea port at Payra has been included, but at this stage, traffic through the port is minimal.

Table A1.4: SASEC Road Corridor 4

Project No.	Project Name	Estimated Cost ($ million)	Status
NEP-RD-01	Upgrading of Kathmandu–Naubise–Mugling road	257.00	Project planned and funding identified, which may or may not be finalized
NEP-RD 02	Upgrading of Mugling–Narayanghat highway	310.00	Project completed or under implementation
NEP-RD-03	Upgrading of Pathlaiya–Hetauda–Narayanghat road	220.00	Project planned and funding identified, which may or may not be finalized
NEP-RD-04	Construction of a new 4-lane expressway from Kathmandu to Nijgadh	1,200.00	Project planned and funding identified, which may or may not be finalized
NEP-RD-06	Upgrading of Dhalkebar–Pathlaiya section	200.00	Project completed or under implementation
NEP-RD-07	Upgrading of Kamala–Dhalkebar section	50.00	Project planned and funding identified, which may or may not be finalized

continued next page

Table A1.4: *Continued*

Project No.	Project Name	Estimated Cost ($ million)	Status
NEP-RD-08	Upgrading of Kanchanpur–Kamala section	180.00	Project completed or under implementation
NEP-RD-09	Upgrading of Kakarvitta–Laukahi section	250.00	Project planned and funding identified, which may or may not be finalized
NEP-RD-10	Upgrading of national highway between Mugling and Pokhara	175.00	Project planned and funding identified, which may or may not be finalized
IND-RD-42	Mechi Bridge on India–Nepal border	16.00	Project completed or under implementation
IND-RD-43	Upgrading of Panitanki–Fulbari border link roads	63.00	Project completed or under implementation
IND-RD-40	Upgrading of Jaigaon–Pasakha border–Changrabandha border link road	89.00	Project completed or under implementation
IND-RD-41	Construction of Pasakha Access Road	10.00	Project completed or under implementation
BAN-RD-15	Improvement of Rangpur–Banglabandha road	1,500.00	Project planned and funding identified, which may or may not be finalized
BAN-RD-16	Improvement of Burimari–Rangpur road	1,450.00	Project planned and funding identified, which may or may not be finalized
BAN-RD-17	Improvement of Elenga–Hatikamrul–Rangpur road section	1,600.00	Project completed or under implementation
BAN-RD-18	Upgrading of Elenga–Joydevpur road section	417.00	Project completed or under implementation
BAN-RD-19	Greater Dhaka Sustainable Urban Transport Project (BRT Gazipur–Airport)	245.00	Project completed or under implementation
BAN-RD-20	Upgrading of Bogra–Natore Road	400.00	Project planned but no funding identified
BAN-RD-21	Improvement of Hatikamrul–Bonpara–Jhenaidah road sections	1,000.00	Project planned and funding identified, which may or may not be finalized
BAN-RD-22	Upgrading of Jhenaidah–Jessore–Khulna road	270.00	Project planned and funding identified, which may or may not be finalized
BAN-RD-23	Upgrading of Khulna–Mongla road	143.00	Project planned but no funding identified
BAN-RD-24	Improvement of Daulatdia–Magura–Jhenaidah–Jessore–Khulna Road	955.00	Project planned but no funding identified
BAN-RD-25	Bhanga–Barisal–Kuakala with connection to Payra Port	1,300.00	Project planned and funding identified, which may or may not be finalized

BAN = Bangladesh, IND = India, NEP = Nepal, RD = road, SASEC = South Asia Subregional Economic Cooperation.

Sources: Asian Development Bank; country submissions in 2018.

SASEC Road Corridor 5: "North Bangladesh–India Connector": Dhaka–Sylhet–Tamabil–Dawki–Shillong–Guwahati (480 km), including 5a spur to Sheola–Sutarkandi–Silchar (114 km)

SASEC Corridor 5 is a short-distance link running northeast from Dhaka to the important "Chicken's Neck" (Corridor 2) region. The Dhaka–Sylhet section is a busy 2-lane road between the capital and the regional capital in the northeast of Bangladesh. There is significant passenger and freight traffic, the latter including material transshipped at the Tamabil border. The road from Sylhet to the Tamabil border is dominated by cross-border passenger traffic and coal and stones coming from across the border. The coal originates from mines in and across Meghalaya and is mainly destined for brickworks across Bangladesh, but mostly around Dhaka. The stones come mainly from the same region, but some from as far away as Bhutan. The roads are to be widened on both sides of the border. However, the main constraint at present is the Dawki suspension bridge, which has a low weight limit, that compels trucks to off-load part of their cargo to be portered across the bridge and then be reloaded on the other side. From Dawki, the road climbs through the Khasi Jaintia Hills toward Shillong. Given the terrain, even 2-laning is likely to be difficult and may take some years to complete. The road from Shillong to Guwahati is a busy commercial road that recently has been converted to a 4-lane highway. The 5b spur road, which links Sylhet with the Indian border to the east toward Silchar, is in poor condition but improves on the Indian side west of Karimganj. This is not a busy freight route at this stage but could grow as through-transport is allowed and provide Bangladesh with access through to northern Myanmar via Imphal.

Table A1.5: SASEC Road Corridor 5

Project No.	Project Name	Estimated Cost ($ million)	Status
BAN-RD-26	Upgrading of Dhaka–Sylhet Highway	1,349.00	Project planned but no finding identified
BAN-RD-27	Improvement of Sylhet–Tamabil road	435.00	Project planned and funding identified, which may or may not be finalized
BAN-RD-28	Improvement of Sylhet–Sheola–Sutarkandi road	250.00	Project planned but no finding identified
IND-RD-44	Upgrading of Dawki to Shillong road including rehabilitation of Dawki bridge at border	186.00	Project planned and funding identified, which may or may not be finalized
IND-RD-C10	Upgrading of the Shillong–Guwahati road	NA	Project completed or under implementation

NA = not available, BAN = Bangladesh, IND = India, RD = road, SASEC = South Asia Subregional Economic Cooperation.
Sources: Asian Development Bank; country submissions in 2018.

SASEC Road Corridor 6: "Sri Lanka Port Highway": Colombo–Kurunegala–Dambulla–Trincomalee (249 km), including 6a: Kurunegala–Kandy spur (33 km)

SASEC Corridor 6 connects Sri Lanka's chief port with the north of the island and its main port facing India. The spur to Kandy is important as it is both a regional and tourist center located off the Central Expressway. The Central Expressway project was intended to connect Colombo with the central north of the island, with a spur connection to Kandy. This covered some of the busiest road sections on the route north from Colombo and would link into the city bypass north of the airport. The People's Republic of China (PRC) had offered funding assistance for the project and is committed to funding of Stage II and construction has commenced. Work on Stage I has been suspended, and Stage III is being developed with possible alternate funding. Stage IV remains unfunded, but India has offered to fund upgrading of the Dambulla–Trincomalee section, though construction has yet to commence. The two projects in Colombo city relate to improving access to the port and separating this traffic stream from city traffic. The first project, the Kelani Bridge development is under construction. Work on the elevated highway has not yet commenced because it links into the Kelani Bridge development that will not be completed until 2020 and as also because it is currently unfunded.

Table A1.6: SASEC Road Corridor 6

Project No.	Project Name	Estimated Cost ($ million)	Status
SL-RD-01	Construction of Central Expressway	1,000.00	Project planned and funding identified, which may or may not be finalized
SL-RD-02	Construction of Central Expressway	952.00	Project completed or under implementation
SL-RD-03	Construction of Central Expressway	500.00	Project planned and funding identified, which may or may not be finalized
SL-RD-04	Construction of Central Expressway	1,000.00	Project planned and funding identified, which may or may not be finalized
SL-RD-05	Development of road sections from Dambulla to Trincomalee	540.00	Project planned and funding identified, which may or may not be finalized
SL-RD-C01	Development of Kurunegala–Trincomalee Road		Project completed or under implementation
SL-RD-06	Construction of city links to Colombo Port	100.00	Project completed or under implementation
SL-RD-07	Elevated toll highway between the New Kelani Bridge (NKB) and port gate	593.00	Project completed or under implementation

RD = road, SASEC = South Asia Subregional Economic Cooperation, SL = Sri Lanka.

Sources: Asian Development Bank; country submissions in 2018.

APPENDIX 2

SASEC RAILWAY CORRIDORS FOR THE SASEC OPERATIONAL PLAN

SASEC Railway Corridor 1: "Nepal–Kolkata Trade Corridor":
Birgunj–Raxaul–Muzaffarpur–Patna–Gaya–Asansol–Kolkata–Haldia (910 km)

SASEC Rail Corridor 1 is the key trade route linking landlocked Nepal with its largest trading partner, India, as well as for trade with third countries passing through Kolkata Port or Haldia Port. The eastern half of the corridor follows the main New Delhi–Kolkata line and becomes increasingly congested with both freight and passengers sharing track. This results in limitations of train paths through to Nepal, as well as to other inland destinations from Kolkata. The strategy is to increase the corridor's capacity to handle additional freight train paths. No information is available on changes to rail tracks in this Corridor. Occasionally, trains are routed through different sections of track and thus the above routing may differ at times.

SASEC Railway Corridor 2: "India–Bangladesh Rail Corridor": Kolkata–Ranaghat–Gede–Tangail
–Dhaka–Cumilla–Chattogram (Chittagong)–Cox's Bazar (675 km), including spur line 2a:
Cumilla–Agartala–Akhaura (57 km); 2b: links to northwest Bangladesh (79 km and 156 km);
2c: Darshana–Khulna–Mongla (150 km); and 2d: connections to Payra Port (236 km)

SASEC Railway Corridor 2 is the main railway link between India and Bangladesh at both the western end (Gede–Darshana) and the eastern end through the Akhaura–Agartala link under development. It includes the busy trade corridor between Dhaka and its main port, Chattogram, and the extension south to Cox's Bazar, which may eventually link through to Myanmar. The other spur lines link the northwest part of the country with its seaports. The strategy is to both increase railway capacity and the ability to handle broad-gauge freight trains.

Table A2: SASEC Railway Corridors 1 and 2

Project No.	Project Name	Estimated Cost ($ million)	Status
IND-RW-01	Birgunj–Kolkata	NA	Project completed or under implementation
BAN-RW-01	Double tracking Ishwardi–Bangabandhu Bridge section	1,701.00	Project planned and funding identified, which may or may not be finalized
BAN-RW-02	Construction of a second Bangabandhu Bridge	1,173.00	Project planned and funding identified, which may or may not be finalized
BAN-RW-03	New Dual gauging of Sirajganj–Bogra railway line	796.00	Project planned and funding identified, which may or may not be finalized

continued next page

Table A2: *Continued*

Project No.	Project Name	Estimated Cost ($ million)	Status
BAN-RW-04	Construction of dual-gauge second line from Abdulpur to Parbatipur	NA	Project planned but no funding identified
BAN-RW-05	Double tracking section of Joydevpur–Tongi section	133.35	Project planned but no funding identified
BAN-RW-06	Double tracking Tongi–Dhaka section	133.35	Project planned but no funding identified
BAN-RW-07	Conversion of existing meter gauge double line to dual gauge between Tongi and Bhairab	NA	Project planned but no funding identified
BAN-RW-08	Dual gauging of line between Akhaura and Laksham	784.00	Project completed or under implementation
BAN-RW-09	Conversion of meter gauge double line to dual gauge between Bhairab Bazar and Akhaura, and rebuilding of the existing Bhairab and Titas old bridge	NA	Project planned but no funding identified
BAN-RW-10	New railway link Akhaura–Agartala (Bangladesh portion)	58.00	Project completed or under implementation
BAN-RW-11	Conversion of existing meter gauge double line to dual gauge between Laksam and Chattogram	NA	Project planned but no funding identified
BAN-RW-12	Construction of double-track, high-speed railway from Dhaka to Chattogram via Cumilla–Laksham	NA	Project planned but no funding identified
BAN-RW-13	Construction of second rail-road bridge on Karnapuli River	241.00	Project planned and funding identified, which may or may not be finalized
BAN-RW-14	Chattogram–Cox's Bazar–Gundum Rail Line construction	2,373.00	Project completed or under implementation
BAN-RW-15	Construction of broad-gauge, double-track line in section between Khulna and Darshana junction	446.00	Project planned and funding identified, which may or may not be finalized
BAN-RW-16	Construction of Khulna–Mongla Port railway line	458.00	Project planned and funding identified, which may or may not be finalized
BAN-RW-17	Construction of broad-gauge railway line from Bhanga junction (Faridpur) to Payra Port via Barisal	NA	Project planned but no funding identified

NA = not available, BAN = Bangladesh, IND = India, RW = railway, SASEC = South Asia Subregional Economic Cooperation.

Sources: Asian Development Bank; country submissions in 2018.

APPENDIX 3

SASEC PORTS FOR THE SASEC OPERATIONAL PLAN

Bangladesh has two main ports and two deepwater ports under development. Chattogram Port (formerly Chittagong) handles 98% of Bangladesh's maritime trade and is congested. Mongla Port is in the southwest and is being developed, in part to compensate for the problems at Chattogram and in part as a port for an extended hinterland in the west of the country. Matabari Port is in the southwest near Cox's Bazar and is primarily being developed in connection with a major power plant. Initially designed to handle coal traffic, Matabari Port has the potential to handle other traffic once it is built. In southwest of Dhaka, Payra Port is being developed as a major deepwater port to handle bulk cargoes and, possibly, containers. It is designed to be able to handle deeper drafted vessels than is possible at the other ports and is intended to reduce freight costs due to the economies of scale in their carriage.

Table A3.1: SASEC Ports in Bangladesh

Project No.	Project Name	Estimated Cost ($ million)	Status
BAN-PT-01	Chattogram Port Enhancement Project (including Karnaphully Container Terminal at Chattogram Port)	200.00	Project planned and funding identified, which may or may not be finalized
BAN-PT-02	Upgrading of Chattogram Port: a. New Bay Container Terminal b. Craneage c. Laldia Multipurpose/Bulk Terminal	2,772.00	Project planned and funding identified, which may or may not be finalized
BAN-PT-03	Patenga Container Terminal	220.00	Project completed or under implementation
BAN-PT-04	Matabari Port Project	1,500.00	Project planned and funding identified, which may or may not be finalized
BAN-PT-05	Development of Mongla Port	714.83	Project planned and funding identified, which may or may not be finalized
BAN-PT-06	Development of Payra Port a. Project on Payra Port's First Terminal and related facilities development b. Project on Establishment of Payra Port's Multipurpose Terminal c. Capital and Maintenance Dredging of Rabnabad Channel of Payra Port d. Development of a Coal/Bulk Terminal at Payra Port	2,381.00	Project completed or under implementation

BAN = Bangladesh, PT = port, SASEC = South Asia Subregional Economic Cooperation.

Sources: Asian Development Bank; country submissions in 2018.

In **India**, Chennai is the largest port in terms of container handling, but its growth is constrained by competition from neighboring "minor ports"—Kattupalli and Krishnapatnam—and service constraints, particularly regarding the landside interface. Thoothukudi is the most southerly port and its overall tonnage throughput has been falling, despite increased container traffic. Visakhapatanam is the largest port on the east coast in terms of tonnage throughput due to its major traffic flows of bulk cargoes but is also growing as a container port. Similarly, Paradip is mainly a bulk cargo port, but with a few container movements. Kolkata is mainly a container and "clean" cargo port, whereas Haldia is principally an industrial port handling bulk cargoes and some containers. Kolkata is the main container port but suffers from the usual problems associated with being a "city" port with congested landside interfaces.

Table A3.2: SASEC Ports in India

Project No.	Project Name	Estimated Cost ($ million)	Status
IND-PT-01	Expansion of Inner Harbor at Paradip Port	226.00	Project planned and funding identified, which may or may not be finalized
IND-PT-02	Development of Outer Harbor nearer to south of South Breakwater at Paradip Port	2,454.00	Project planned and funding identified, which may or may not be finalized
IND-PT-03	Haldia Port Upgrading: a. Augmentation of Capacity of Dock Complex b. Construction of 3 new berths	295.00	Project planned and funding identified, which may or may not be finalized
IND-PT-04	V.O. Chidambaranagar Port Trust, Thoothukudi	462.00	Project planned and funding identified, which may or may not be finalized

IND = India, PT = port, SASEC = South Asia Subregional Economic Cooperation.
Sources: Asian Development Bank; country submissions in 2018.

Colombo is the largest port in **Sri Lanka** and is a major international container hub handling approximately 7 million twenty-foot equivalent units per year. The port consists of an inner and outer harbor (Southern Harbor Extension). Mega container ships can only access the new outer harbor if transiting with maximum draft. Hambantota is a new port in the south, currently handling roll-on/roll-off vessels. Trincomalee is a large harbor with an undeveloped port. There is a plan to construct new facilities based on PPP mode, but no Indian company has expressed interest on this project, hence no decision has been made at this stage.

Table A3.3: SASEC Ports in Sri Lanka

Project No.	Project Name	Estimated Cost ($ million)	Status
SL-PT-01	Completion and Equipping of Eastern Terminal	430.00	Project planned but no funding identified
SL-PT-02	Construction of Western Terminal	600.00	Project planned but no funding identified
SL-PT-03	SASEC Port and Logistics Development Project	200.00	Project planned and funding identified, which may or may not be finalized

PT = port, SASEC = South Asia Subregional Economic Cooperation, SL = Sri Lanka.
Sources: Asian Development Bank; country submissions in 2018.

APPENDIX 4

SASEC AIRPORTS FOR THE SASEC OPERATIONAL PLAN

Bangladesh has four international airports in Dhaka, Chattogram, Sylhet, and Cox's Bazar. The main airport is Hazrat Shahjalal International Airport located in Dhaka. Due to increased traffic, the airport is in need of expanding its capacity to handle more passengers and cargo. The upgrade, which includes building a second terminal, has already commenced and will be completed by 2022. Because traffic buildup is expected to cause further landing and take-off delays, the construction of a second parallel runway is under consideration. Longer-term planning includes a new Dhaka airport—Bangabandhu Sheikh Mujib International Airport—but this is only at an early planning stage. In Chattogram, the Shah Amanat Airport requires runway strengthening to be able to accommodate Boeing 777 aircraft being used by Biman Bangladesh Airways, among other carriers. Work is due to commence imminently, but upgrades to the passenger terminal and a second runway are only at an early programming stage. A project to strengthen the runway at Sylhet Osmani International Airport is under implementation, but upgrades to the passenger terminal are only at programming stage. Cox's Bazar, the latest international airport, is having its runway strengthened and its passenger facilities upgraded.

Table A4.1: SASEC Airports in Bangladesh

Project No.	Project Name	Estimated Cost ($ million)	Status
BAN-AP-01	Third passenger terminal at Hazrat Shahjalal International Airport, Dhaka	1,660.00	Project completed or under implementation
BAN-AP-02	Upgrading of Hazrat Shahjalal International Airport, Dhaka: a. Airport safety and security system improvement b. Expansion and strengthening of cargo apron	46.00	Project completed or under implementation
BAN-AP-03	Development of Cox's Bazar International Airport	143.00	Project completed or under implementation

AP = airport, BAN = Bangladesh, SASEC = South Asia Subregional Economic Cooperation.

Sources: Asian Development Bank; country submissions in 2018.

Bhutan has only one international airport which is located in Paro district. Paro Airport, which is located deep in a valley surrounded by mountains, is suitable only for certain types of jet aircraft and has restricted operating hours. The airport has a modern passenger terminal built to traditional design. The runway could be widened but not extended due to topographic restrictions. A parallel taxiway is being constructed to enable more efficient use of the runway during the limited operating hours, while extension of the departures terminal is also underway. Upgrading plans include widening of the runway for the A319/320 operated by Druk Air and constructing a dedicated cargo facility.

Table A4.2: SASEC Airports in Bhutan

Project No.	Project Name	Estimated Cost ($ million)	Status
BHU-AP-01	Upgrading Paro Airport: a. Runway widening b. Construction of modern cargo terminal	55.00	Project planned and funding identified, which may or may not be finalized
BHU-AP-02	Paro Airport: Construction of parallel taxiway and re-modification of departure terminal building	2.00	Project completed or under implementation
BHU-AP-03	Expansion of Gelephu Airport	200.00	Project planned but no funding identified

AP = airport, BHU = Bhutan, SASEC = South Asia Subregional Economic Cooperation.

Sources: Asian Development Bank; country submissions in 2018.

India has two main airports along its SASEC east coast—Chennai and Kolkata. The airport in Chennai was modernized and expanded in 2012 but is reaching full capacity. To address this issue, construction of a new domestic terminal and expansion of the international terminal are both ongoing. Proposals for the construction of a new airport for Chennai are still in the early planning stage. In 2013, Kolkata Airport opened its new integrated passenger terminal with a capacity of 23 million passengers per year. The old and new terminals need to be interconnected to cope with increased traffic flows and for improved efficiency. The plan is to construct a new domestic terminal, thereby releasing more capacity for international traffic and more space for domestic carriers. Other developments are taking place to increase the capacities of Thoothukudi and Guwahati airports.

Table A4.3: SASEC Airports in India

Project No.	Project Name	Estimated Cost ($ million)	Status
IND-AP-01	Chennai Airport Expansion Program	335.00	Project completed or under implementation
IND-AP-02	Guwahati Airport	186.00	Project completed or under implementation

AP = airport, IND = India, SASEC = South Asia Subregional Economic Cooperation.

Sources: Country submissions; ADB consultant's report.

Myanmar's main international airport is in Yangon. Due to the rapid increase in passenger traffic in recent years, the airport's facilities are congested. Terminal 2 has been taken out of operation for extensive renovation and upgrading. Scheduled for reopening in 2019, Terminal 2 is expected to significantly increase the airport's handling capacity. The international airports in Mandalay and Nay Pyi Taw are both modern but underutilized, whereas the Yangon airport is operating at overcapacity. In response, the government has planned to construct a greenfield airport near Bago, to be called Hanthawaddy International Airport. The project has been delayed several times, but construction of the greenfield airport is projected to commence in 2019.

Table A4.4: SASEC Airports in Myanmar

Project No.	Project Name	Estimated Cost ($ million)	Status
MYA-AP-01	Renovation of Terminal 2 (T2) at Yangon International Airport	666.00	Project completed or under implementation
MYA-AP-02	Hanthawaddy International Airport	1,812.00	Project planned and funding identified, which may or may not finalized
MYA-AP-03	Development of new cargo terminal at Mandalay International Airport	5.00	Project completed or under implementation

AP = airport, MYA = Myanmar, SASEC = South Asia Subregional Economic Cooperation.

Sources: Asian Development Bank; country submissions in 2018.

Nepal's Tribhuvan International Airport is in the center of Kathmandu and is the country's principal international airport. As traffic increased, so has congestion, particularly in the international terminal. A new domestic terminal has been completed, and some initial remedial work has been undertaken on the international terminal. However, the runway needs extending to be able to accommodate larger aircraft and equipment provided to address the country's poor safety record. In addition, the international terminal requires a more substantial upgrade, and detailed design plans have been submitted. There are plans to develop a greenfield international airport at Nijgadh in the lowlands south of the mountain ranges, but the project remains in the planning phase. Other projects are the expansion and upgrading of the Gautam Buddha Airport in Bhairahawa and construction of a new airport in Pokhara.

Table A4.5: SASEC Airports in Nepal

Project No.	Project Name	Estimated Cost ($ million)	Status
NEP-AP-01	Tribhuvan International Airport Capacity Enhancement Sector Development Program	220.00	Project planned and funding identified, which may or may not be finalized
NEP-AP-02	Expansion and upgrading of Gautam Buddha Airport, about 280 kilometers west of Kathmandu	65.00	Project completed or under implementation

AP = airport, NEP = Nepal, SASEC = South Asia Subregional Economic Cooperation.

Sources: Asian Development Bank; country submissions in 2018.

Sri Lanka has two international airports. The major airport is the Bandaranaike International Airport located in the northern suburbs of Colombo. The facility acts as a "mini-hub" for connections to Maldives, in addition to its point-to-point flights and being the base for SriLankan Airlines. Current traffic is approximately 10 million passengers per year, and the airport has been gradually upgraded. To date, existing passenger terminals have been rehabilitated and the main runway has had an overlay, but a larger program is underway to expand the airport buildings and aprons/taxiways. The second airport is the Mattala Rajapaksa International Airport in the south which has been developed with funding from the PRC. Unfortunately, it has not attracted any carriers and is incurring significant losses. India has indicated an interest in a joint venture to take over the airport, but no decisions have been made.

Table A4.6: SASEC Airports in Sri Lanka

Project No.	Project Name	Estimated Cost ($ million)	Status
SRI-AP-01	Bandaranaike International Airport Development Phase II Stage II	550.00	Project completed or under implementation

AP = airport, SASEC = South Asia Subregional Economic Cooperation, SRI = Sri Lanka.

Sources: Asian Development Bank; country submissions in 2018.

APPENDIX 5

SASEC OPERATIONAL PLAN TRANSPORT PROJECTS – BY COUNTRY

Table A5.1a: SASEC Road Projects in Bangladesh

Project No. BAN-RD-01	
Project Name: Benapole–Jessore road	
Project Snapshot/Description: AH1 – 38 km: Upgrading of Benapole highway to 4 lanes	
Estimated Cost ($ million): 41.00	
Indicative Funding Source: Government of Bangladesh	
SASEC Road Corr #: 2	
Status: Project completed or under implementation	
SASEC OP: OP-1 (i)	
Project No. BAN-RD-02	
Project Name: New alignment of AH1 Bhanga–Narail–Jessore–Benapole road	
Project Snapshot/Description: New AH1 – 137 km: Upgrading to 4-lane highway to connect Indian border with the new Padma Multipurpose Bridge Approach Alignment	
Estimated Cost ($ million): 920.00	
Indicative Funding Source: Government of Bangladesh and Government of India (TBC)	
SASEC Road Corr #: 2	
Status: Project planned and funding identified, which may or may not be finalized	
SASEC OP: OP-1 (i)	
Remarks: Proposed for Indian Line of Credit financing (TBC). FS and DPR ongoing under the Subregional Transport Project Preparatory Facility (SRTPPF-II) project.	
Project No. BAN-RD-03	
Project Name: New Padma Bridge	
Project Snapshot/Description: AH1 – 9 km: Construction of new multipurpose bridge will a length of 6.1 km with viaduct of 3 km	
Estimated Cost ($ million): 2,900.00	
Indicative Funding Source: Government of Bangladesh	
SASEC Road Corr #: 2	
Status: Project completed or under implementation	
SASEC OP: OP-1 (i)	
Remarks: The total cost of BAN-RD-03 and BAN-RD-04 is $3,900 million.	

continued next page

Table A5.1a: *Continued*

Project No. BAN-RD-04

Project Name: New Padma Bridge approach roads

Project Snapshot/Description: 11 km of approach road south end from Janjira to Bridge and 1.6 km to Mawa from the southern end

Estimated Cost ($ million): 1,000.00

Indicative Funding Source: Government of Bangladesh

SASEC Road Corr #: 2

Status: Project completed or under implementation

SASEC OP: OP-1 (i)

Remarks: The total cost of BAN-RD-03 and BAN-RD-04 is $3,900 million.

Project No. BAN-RD-05

Project Name: Northern link road

Project Snapshot/Description: 55 km: Construction of 4-lane link road between Mawa and Dhaka

Estimated Cost ($ million): 860.00

Indicative Funding Source: Government of Bangladesh

SASEC Road Corr #: 2

Status: Project completed or under implementation

SASEC OP: OP-1 (i)

Project No. BAN-RD-06

Project Name: Construction of the Dhaka Elevated Expressway

Project Snapshot/Description: Uninterrupted road connection between the Dhaka–Chattogram Highway and the Dhaka–Tangail–Hatikamrul Highway through the proposed Dhaka–Ashulia elevated expressway along AH2

Estimated Cost ($ million): 1,132.00

Indicative Funding Source: PPP

SASEC Road Corr #: 2

Status: Project completed or under implementation

SASEC OP: OP-1 (i)

Project No. BAN-RD-07

Project Name: Construction of the Dhaka–Ashulia Elevated Expressway

Project Snapshot/Description: Uninterrupted road connection between the Dhaka–Chattogram Highway and the Dhaka–Tangail–Hatikamral Highway through the ongoing Dhaka Elevated Expressway along A12

Estimated Cost ($ million): 2,098.00

Indicative Funding Source: Government of Bangladesh and Government of the PRC

SASEC Road Corr #: 2

Status: Project completed or under implementation

SASEC OP: OP-1 (i)

continued next page

Table A5.1a: *Continued*

Project No. BAN-RD-08
Project Name: Construction of the Dhaka East–West Elevated Expressway

Project Snapshot/Description: Linking of the Dhaka–Aricha Highway (NH 5) and the Dhaka-Chattogram Highway (NH 1) with a connection to the Dhaka–Mawa Highway, which links directly with the Padma Bridge

Estimated Cost ($ million): 2,049.00

Indicative Funding Source: Government of Bangladesh and Government of Malaysia

SASEC Road Corr #: 2

Status: Project completed or under implementation

SASEC OP: OP-1 (i)

Project No. BAN-RD-09
Project Name: Kanchpur, Meghna, and Gumpti bridges

Project Snapshot/Description: Construction of new 4-lane Kanchpur, Meghna, and Gumpti 2nd bridges and existing bridge rehabilitation

Estimated Cost ($ million): 1,061.00

Indicative Funding Source: Government of Bangladesh and JICA

SASEC Road Corr #: 2

Status: Project completed or under implementation

SASEC OP: OP-1 (i)

Project No. BAN-RD-10
Project Name: Rehabilitation of Baraierhat-Heako-Ramgarh roads

Project Snapshot/Description: R151/2 – 50 km: Upgrading of roads to Asian Highway Class II

Estimated Cost ($ million): 100.00

Indicative Funding Source: Government of Bangladesh, Government of India (TBC), and JICA

SASEC Road Corr #: 2

Status: Project planned and funding identified, which may or may not be finalized

SASEC OP: OP-1 (iii)

Remarks: Important feeder road into northeastern states of India. DPR completed, including financial plan for Indian Line of Credit (LOC) (TBC). JICA to fund construction of eight bridges.

Project No. BAN-RD-11
Project Name: Chattogram Port Access Road Improvement

Project Snapshot/Description: 12 km: Construction of 6-lane road, providing last mile connectivity to Chattogram Port from the Dhaka–Chattogram highway

Estimated Cost ($ million): 150.00

Indicative Funding Source: TBD

SASEC Road Corr #: 2

Status: Project planned but no funding identified

SASEC OP: OP-1 (iii)

Table A5.1a: *Continued*

Project No. BAN-RD-12
Project Name: Construction of new Dhaka–Chattogram Expressway on PPP basis

Project Snapshot/Description: Expressway to be undertaken in three packages and includes construction of 218 km, 4-lane highway with provision for 6 lanes, construction of service roads and two major bridges

Estimated Cost ($ million): 2,750.00

Indicative Funding Source: PPP

SASEC Road Corr #: 2

Status: Project planned and funding identified, which may or may not be finalized

SASEC OP: OP-1 (i)

Remarks: FS/DD to be completed under ADB loan. Viability Gap Funding is approved and tenders to be floated.

Project No. BAN-RD-13
Project Name: Karnaphuli Multi-Channel Tunnel Project

Project Snapshot/Description: 9 km: Tunnel will connect the port city of Chattogram to the far side of the Karnaphuli River, the site of a new PRC-supported economic zone

Estimated Cost ($ million): 1,250.00

Indicative Funding Source: Government of Bangladesh and Government of the PRC

SASEC Road Corr #: 2

Status: Project completed or under implementation

SASEC OP: OP-1 (iii)

Remarks: Export–Import Bank of China has provided $706.00 million. The outstanding balance to be provided by the Government of Bangladesh.

Project No. BAN-RD-14
Project Name: Improvement of Chattogram–Cox's Bazar Highway through PPP

Project Snapshot/Description: AH41 – 136 km: Upgrade Class II roads to 4-lane Class I as potential future link to Myanmar via Teknaf

Estimated Cost ($ million): 1,700.00

Indicative Funding Source: PPP (Government to Government with Japan)

SASEC Road Corr #: 2

Status: Project planned and funding identified, which may or may not be finalized

SASEC OP: OP-1 (i)

continued next page

Table A5.1a: *Continued*

Project No. BAN-RD-15
Project Name: Improvement of Rangpur–Banglabandha road

Project Snapshot/Description: NH5 – 202 km: Upgrade of road to 4-lane highway from Rangpur to Banglabandha border with India

Estimated Cost ($ million): 1,500.00

Indicative Funding Source: Government of Bangladesh and ADB

SASEC Road Corr #: 4

Status: Project planned and funding identified, which may or may not be finalized

SASEC OP: OP-1 (i)

Remarks: Draft FS/DD has been submitted to Government by the consultants under the ADB project Subregional Transport Project Preparatory Facility (SRTPPF-II) (Loan 3295).

Project No. BAN-RD-16
Project Name: Improvement of Rangpur–Burimari road

Project Snapshot/Description: N5/N506/N509/Feeder Road (LGED) – 160 km of Rangpur–Tista–Kakina road (58 km) to 4-lane and Rangpur–Mohipur–Kakina road (102 km) to 4-lane with service lane

Estimated Cost ($ million): 1,450.00

Indicative Funding Source: Government of Bangladesh and ADB

SASEC Road Corr #: 4

Status: Project planned and funding identified, which may or may not be finalized

SASEC OP: OP-1 (i)

Remarks: FS/DD of Rangpur–Burimari road completed with ADB financing. FS/DD of Rangpur–Mohipur–Kakina road is being processed. This is part of corridor 4a spur road.

Project No. BAN-RD-17
Project Name: Improvement of Elenga–Hatikamrul–Rangpur road section

Project Snapshot/Description: N514/405 – 190 km: Road being improved to 2 lanes, later to 4 lanes

Estimated Cost ($ million): 1,600.00

Indicative Funding Source: Government of Bangladesh and ADB

SASEC Road Corr #: 4

Status: Project completed or under implementation

SASEC OP: OP-1 (ii)

Remarks: Included in the ADB project Dhaka–Northwest Corridor Road Project with ADB financing of $300 million (Loan 3592/3593)

continued next page

Table A5.1a: *Continued*

Project No. BAN-RD-18
Project Name: Upgrading of Elenga–Joydevpur road section

Project Snapshot/Description: N4 – 69 km: Road being upgraded to 4 lanes

Estimated Cost ($ million): 417.00

Indicative Funding Source: Government of Bangladesh and ADB

SASEC Road Corr #: 4

Status: Project completed or under implementation

SASEC OP: OP-1 (i)

Remarks: Project part of the project SASEC Road Connectivity Project with ADB financing of $198 million (Loan 2949)

Project No. BAN-RD-19
Project Name: Greater Dhaka Sustainable Urban Transport project (BRT Gazipur – Airport)

Project Snapshot/Description: N3 – 16 km: Improvement of highway from 4- to 6-lane highway past airport

Estimated Cost ($ million): 245.00

Indicative Funding Source: Government of Bangladesh and ADB

SASEC Road Corr #: 4

Status: Project completed or under implementation

SASEC OP: OP-1 (i)

Remarks: Part of the project Greater Dhaka Sustainable Urban Transport Project with ADB financing of $160 million (Loan 2862/2863/2864).

Project No. BAN-RD-20
Project Name: Upgrading of Bogra–Natore Road

Project Snapshot/Description: N502 – 67 km: Upgrade of 2-lane road to 4 lanes at later stage

Estimated Cost ($ million): 400.00

Indicative Funding Source: TBD

SASEC Road Corr #: 4

Status: Project planned but no funding identified

SASEC OP: OP-1 (ii)

Remarks: Cost estimate by consultant. This is part of corridor 4b spur road.

continued next page

Table A5.1a: *Continued*

Project No. BAN-RD-21
Project Name: Improvement of Hatikamrul–Bonpara–Jhenaidah road sections
Project Snapshot/Description: N507/N6/N704/N705 – 170 km: Upgrading of 2 lane sections followed by 4-laning at later stage
Estimated Cost ($ million): 1,000.00
Indicative Funding Source: Government of Bangladesh and World Bank
SASEC Road Corr #: 4
Status: Project planned and funding identified, which may or may not be finalized
SASEC OP: OP-1 (ii)
Remarks: FS/DD of Natore-Bonpara road section prepared under ADB's SRTPPF project. FS/DD of Bonpara–Jhenaidah road is ongoing under SRTPPF-II project (Loan 3295). This is part of corridor 4b spur road.
Project No. BAN-RD-22
Project Name: Upgrading of Jhenaidah–Jessore–Khulna road
Project Snapshot/Description: N7 – 46 km: Upgrading of existing 2-lane sections of Jhenaidah–Jessore road into 4 lanes
Estimated Cost ($ million): 270.00
Indicative Funding Source: Government of Bangladesh and World Bank
SASEC Road Corr #: 4
Status: Project planned and funding identified, which may or may not be finalized
SASEC OP: OP-1 (ii)
Remarks: DPR has been prepared for Jessore–Khulna–Mongla sections with ADB funding assistance (SRTPPF-II Loan 3295). This is part of corridor 4b spur road.
Project No. BAN-RD-23
Project Name: Upgrading of Khulna–Mongla road
Project Snapshot/Description: Khulna–Mongla Highway – 37 km: Upgrading with widening to 4 lanes
Estimated Cost ($ million): 143.00
Indicative Funding Source: TBD
SASEC Road Corr #: 4
Status: Project planned but no funding identified
SASEC OP: OP-1 (ii)
Remarks: FS/DD completed with ADB financing. This is part of corridor 4b spur road.

continued next page

Table A5.1a: *Continued*

Project No. BAN-RD-24
Project Name: Improvement of Daulatdia–Magura–Jhenaidah–Jessore–Khulna road

Project Snapshot/Description: N7/AH1 – 212 km: Improvement to road connecting Dhaka with the Mongla seaport. The project will involve upgrading of existing road to a 4-lane highway, with safety features

Estimated Cost ($ million): 955.00

Indicative Funding Source: TBD

SASEC Road Corr #: 4

Status: Project planned but no funding identified

SASEC OP: OP-1 (iii)

Remarks: This road is an important feeder road to national highway N7 and part of Asian Highway Network (AH1) connecting Dhaka with Mongla Port through Daulatdia ferry ghat and Land Port at Jessore. Economic feeder road to SASEC Road Corridor 4B. This is part of corridor 4b spur road.

Project No. BAN-RD-25
Project Name: Bhanga–Barisal– Kuakala with connection to Payra Port

Project Snapshot/Description: N8/R880/R881 – 236 km: Entails improvement of the Bhanga–Barisal–Kuakala section with connection through to Payra Port.

Estimated Cost ($ million): 1,300.00

Indicative Funding Source: ADB and Government of Bangladesh

SASEC Road Corr #: 4

Status: Project planned and funding identified, which may or may not be finalized

SASEC OP: OP-1 (iii)

Remarks: Complementary to SASEC Road Corridor 4 and 4b leading to ports
ADB will finance Bhanga–Barisal road section. This is part of corridor 4c spur road.

Project No. BAN-RD-26
Project Name: Upgrading of Dhaka–Sylhet Highway

Project Snapshot/Description: N2 – 226 km Dhaka–Sylhet Highway: Improvement to 4-lane highway section road link

Estimated Cost ($ million): 1,349.00

Indicative Funding Source: TBD

SASEC Road Corr #: 5

Status: Project planned but no funding identified

SASEC OP: OP-1 (i)

continued next page

Table A5.1a: *Continued*

Project No. BAN-RD-27
Project Name: Improvement of Sylhet–Tamabil road

Project Snapshot/Description: Improvement of road from 2 lanes to a 4-lane highway

Estimated Cost ($ million): 435.00

Indicative Funding Source: Government of Bangladesh and AIIB

SASEC Road Corr #: 5

Status: Project planned and funding identified, which may or may not be finalized

SASEC OP: OP-1 (i)

Remarks: AIIB funding of $268.00 million has been programmed.

Project No. BAN-RD-28
Project Name: Improvement of Sylhet–Sheola–Sutarkandi road

Project Snapshot/Description: R250 – 43 km: Improvement to 4-lane highway of link road to corridor 4

Estimated Cost ($ million): 250.00

Indicative Funding Source: TBD

SASEC Road Corr #: 5

Status: Project planned but no funding identified

SASEC OP: OP-1 (i)

Remarks: FS/DD and DPR preparation is underway under ADB's TA loan project (SRTPPF-II Loan 3295).

Project No. BAN-RD-29
Project Name: Development of Ashunganj–Akhaura–Agartala road

Project Snapshot/Description: N1/102 – 50 km: Upgrading and 4-laning of key access road to Tripura in the northeast region of India

Estimated Cost ($ million): 430.00

Indicative Funding Source: Government of Bangladesh and Indian LOC

SASEC Road Corr #: 2

Status: Project completed or under implementation

SASEC OP: OP-1 (i)

Remarks: This is part of corridor 2a spur road.

ADB = Asian Development Bank, AIIB = Asian Infrastructure Investment Bank, AH = Asian Highway, BAN = Bangladesh, Corr. = Corridor, DPR = detailed project report, FS/DD = feasibility study/detailed design, JICA = Japan International Cooperation Agency, km = kilometer, NH = national highway, OP = operational plan, PPP = public–private partnership, PRC = People's Republic of China, RD = road, TBC = to be confirmed, TBD = to be determined, SASEC = South Asia Subregional Economic Cooperation, SRTPPF = Subregional Road Transport Project Preparatory Facility (Bangladesh).

Sources: Asian Development Bank; country submissions in 2018.

Table A5.1b: SASEC Railway Projects in Bangladesh

Project No. BAN-RW-01
Project Name: Double tracking Ishwardi–Bangabandhu Bridge section

Project Snapshot/Description: 162.023 km: Construction of Dual-Gauge Main line between Joydevpur–Ishurdi excluding the Bangabandhu Bridge

Estimated Cost ($ million): 1,701.00

Indicative Funding Source: Government of Bangladesh and Government of the PRC

SASEC Road Corr #: 2

Status: Project planned and funding identified, which may or may not be finalized

SASEC OP: OP-2 (i)

Remarks: DPP of the project Construction of Dual Gauge Double Line Between Joydevpur–Ishurdi Section of Bangladesh Railway Line approved for implementation. This project will allow Indian wagons to travel into Bangladesh without the need for transshipment.

Project No. BAN-RW-02
Project Name: Construction of a 2nd Bangabandhu Bridge

Project Snapshot/Description: 4.8 km: Construction of a second bridge over the Jamuna River and Route: 12.527 km

Estimated Cost ($ million): 1,173.00

Indicative Funding Source: Government of Bangladesh and JICA

SASEC Road Corr #: 2

Status: Project planned and funding identified, which may or may not be finalized

SASEC OP: OP-2 (i)

Remarks: Detailed design completed under the project Bangabandhu Sheikh Mujib Railway Bridge Construction.

Project No. BAN-RW-03
Project Name: New Dual Gauge Sirajganj–Bogra railway line

Project Snapshot/Description: 86.51 km: Dual-Gauge New Railway link between Bogra and Sirajganj

Estimated Cost ($ million): 796.00

Indicative Funding Source: Government of Bangladesh and Government of India

SASEC Road Corr #: 2

Status: Project planned and funding identified, which may or may not be finalized

SASEC OP: OP-2 (iii)

Remarks: DPP of the project Construction of DG Rail Link from Bogra to Shahed M. Monsur Ali Station approved for implementation.

It is an important spur line up to the northwest of the country. Project is funded from Indian Line of Credit (LOC).

continued next page

Table A5.1b: *Continued*

Project No. BAN-RW-04

Project Name: Construction of Dual Gauge Second Line from Abdulpur to Parbatipur

Project Snapshot/Description: 157 km: Construction of dual-gauge line between Abdulpur and Parbatipur

Estimated Cost ($ million): TBD

Indicative Funding Source: TBD

SASEC Road Corr #: 2

Status: Project planned but no funding identified

SASEC OP: OP-2 (iii)

Remarks: Another spur line to the northwest. This is a major subregional corridor and key part of Trans-Asian Railway Network. DPR preparation is ongoing. This is part of corridor 2b spur road.

Project No. BAN-RW-05

Project Name: Double tracking section of Joydevpur–Tongi section

Project Snapshot/Description: 11 km: Double tracking of congested railway section near Dhaka where several lines converge

Estimated Cost ($ million): 133.35

Indicative Funding Source: Government of Bangladesh and Government of India (LOC)

SASEC Road Corr #: 2

Status: Project planned but no funding identified

SASEC OP: OP-2 (i)

Remarks: Project is part of the Construction of 3rd and 4th Dual Gauge Line in Dhaki–Tongi and Dual Gauge Double Line in Dhaka–Joydevpur Section of Bangladesh Railway (1st Revised) Project.

Project No. BAN-RW-06

Project Name: Double tracking Tongi–Dhaka section

Project Snapshot/Description: 46 km: Line rehabilitation and addition of third and fourth tracks

Estimated Cost ($ million): 133.35

Indicative Funding Source: Government of Bangladesh and Government of India (LOC)

SASEC Road Corr #: 2

Status: Project planned but no funding identified

SASEC OP: OP-2 (i)

Remarks: Project is part of the Construction of 3rd and 4th Dual Gauge Line in Dhaka–Tongi and Dual Gauge Double Line in Dhaka–Joydevpur Section of Bangladesh Railway (1st Revised).

continued next page

Table A5.1b: *Continued*

Project No.   BAN-RW-07
Project Name: Conversion of existing meter gauge double line to dual gauge between Tongi and Bhairab
Project Snapshot/Description: 64 km: Conversion of existing meter gauge double line to dual gauge between Tongi and Bhairab
Estimated Cost ($ million): TBD
Indicative Funding Source: TBD
SASEC Road Corr #: 2
Status: Project planned but no funding identified
SASEC OP: OP-2 (i)
Remarks: FS/DD is part of component-01 of the project Dhaka–Chittagong–Cox's Bazar Project Preparatory Facility.
Project No.   BAN-RW-08
Project Name: Dual gauging of line between Akhaura and Laksham
Project Snapshot/Description: 72 km: Construction of dual-gauge, double rail line and conversion of existing railway line into dual gauge on main line between Akhaura and Laksham
Estimated Cost ($ million): 784.00
Indicative Funding Source: Government of Bangladesh, ADB, and EIB
SASEC Road Corr #: 2
Status: Project completed or under implementation
SASEC OP: OP-2 (i)
Remarks: Part of the Construction of Dual Gauge Double Rail Line and Conversion of Existing Rail Line into Dual Gauge Between Akhaura and Laksam Project
Project No.   BAN-RW-09
Project Name: Conversion of meter gauge double line to dual gauge between Bhairab Bazar and Akhaura and rebuilding of the existing Bhairab and Titas old bridge
Project Snapshot/Description: 33 km: Conversion of existing meter gauge double line to dual gauge between Bhairab Bazar and Akhaura
Estimated Cost ($ million): TBD
Indicative Funding Source: TBD
SASEC Road Corr #: 2
Status: Project planned but no funding identified
SASEC OP: OP-2 (i)
Remarks: FD/DD is part of component-01 of the Dhaka–Chittagong–Cox's Bazar Project preparatory facility.

continued next page

Table A5.1b: *Continued*

Project No. BAN-RW-10
Project Name: New railway link Akhaura–Agartala

Project Snapshot/Description: 10 km: New railway link Akhaura–Agartala (Bangladesh Portion)

Estimated Cost ($ million): 58.00

Indicative Funding Source: Government of Bangladesh and Government of India

SASEC Road Corr #: 2

Status: Project completed or under implementation

SASEC OP: OP-2 (i)

Remarks: Part of the construction of Akhaura–Agartala Dual Gauge Railway Link (Bangladesh Portion). This will serve as an important cross-border connection into northeastern states of India. This is part of corridor 2a spur road.

Project No. BAN-RW-11
Project Name: Conversion of existing meter gauge double line to dual gauge between Laksam and Chattogram

Project Snapshot/Description: 128 km: Conversion of existing meter gauge double line to dual gauge between Laksam and Chattogram

Estimated Cost ($ million): TBD

Indicative Funding Source: TBD

SASEC Road Corr #: 2

Status: Project planned but no funding identified

SASEC OP: OP-2 (iii)

Remarks: FS/DD is part of component-2 of the Dhaka–Chittagong–Cox's Bazar Project preparatory facility.

Project No. BAN-RW-12
Project Name: Construction of high-speed railway from Dhaka to Chattogram via Cumilla–Laksham

Project Snapshot/Description: About 33 km: Main line for high-speed train from Dhaka to Chattogram via Cumilla/Laksham

Estimated Cost ($ million): TBD

Indicative Funding Source: TBD

SASEC Road Corr #: 2

Status: Project planned but no funding identified

SASEC OP: OP-2 (iii)

Remarks: FS/DD is part of the feasibility study and detail design for construction of high-speed railway from Dhaka to Chattogram via Cumilla/Laksham Project.

continued next page

Table A5.1b: *Continued*

Project No. BAN-RW-13
Project Name: Construction of second rail-road bridge on Karnapuli River

Project Snapshot/Description: 720 m: Rail-road bridge on Karnapuli River

Estimated Cost ($ million): 241.00

Indicative Funding Source: Government of Bangladesh and Korea Eximbank (KEXIM)

SASEC Road Corr #: 2

Status: Project planned and funding identified, which may or may not be finalized

SASEC OP: OP-2 (iii)

Remarks: DPP for the construction of second rail-road bridge on Karnapuli River was sent to Planning Commission for approval.

Project No. BAN-RW-14
Project Name: Chattogram–Cox's Bazar–Gundum Rail Line construction

Project Snapshot/Description: 129 km: Construction of a new single-line, dual-gauge track from Dohazari to Cox's Bazar via Ramu (100 km), and Ramu to Gundum (29 km)

Estimated Cost ($ million): 2,373.00

Indicative Funding Source: Government of Bangladesh and ADB

SASEC Road Corr #: 2

Status: Project completed or under implementation

SASEC OP: OP-2 (iii)

Remarks: Part of the Construction of Single Line Dual Gauge (DG) Railway Track from Dohazari to Cox's Bazar via Ramu and Ramu to Gundum near Myanmar (1st Revised) Project. This project will establish railway connectivity with Cox's Bazar and provide access to the proposed Trans-Asian Railway Corridor.

Project No. BAN-RW-15
Project Name: Construction of broad-gauge double-track line in section between Khulna and Darshana junction

Project Snapshot/Description: 126 km: Construction of broad-gauge double-track line in section between Khulna and Darshana

Estimated Cost ($ million): 446.00

Indicative Funding Source: Government of Bangladesh and Government of India (LOC)

SASEC Road Corr #: 2

Status: Project planned and funding identified, which may or may not be finalized

SASEC OP: OP-2 (iii)

Remarks: Part of the construction of broad-gauge double-track line between Khulna–Darshana junction section. This will improve railway connectivity with India for southwest Bangladesh and access through to Mongla Port. This is part of corridor 2c spur road.

continued next page

Table A5.1b: *Continued*

Project No. BAN-RW-16
Project Name: Construction of Khulna–Mongla Port railway line

Project Snapshot/Description: 65 km: New broad gauge rail line Khulna–Mongla section

Estimated Cost ($ million): 458.00

Indicative Funding Source: Government of Bangladesh and Government of India (LOC)

SASEC Road Corr #: 2

Status: Project planned and funding identified, which may or may not be finalized

SASEC OP: OP-2 (iii)

Remarks: Part of the construction of Khulna–Mongla Port rail line (1st revised). The project will increase freight and passenger capacity as well as improve railway connectivity with India through construction of main line link between Mongla Port and the capital city, Dhaka. This is part of corridor 2c spur road.

Project No. BAN-RW-17
Project Name: Construction of broad-gauge railway line from Bhanga junction (Faridpur) to Payra Port via Barisal

Project Snapshot/Description: About 190 km: New broad gauge rail line Bhanga junction (Faridpur) to Payra Port via Barisal

Estimated Cost ($ million): TBD

Indicative Funding Source: TBD

SASEC Road Corr #: 2

Status: Project planned but no funding identified

SASEC OP: OP-2 (iii)

Remarks: FS/DD is going on under the project Feasibility Study and Detail Design for Construction of Broad-Gauge Railway Line from Bhanga Junction (Faridput) to Payra Port via Barisal. This is part of corridor 2d spur road.

ADB = Asian Development Bank, BAN = Bangladesh, Corr. = Corridor, DPR = detailed project report, FS/DD = feasibility study/ detailed design, JICA = Japan International Cooperation Agency, km = kilometer, RW = railway, OP = operational plan, PRC = People's Republic of China, SASEC = South Asia Subregional Economic Cooperation, TBD = to be determined.

Sources: Asian Development Bank; country submissions in 2018.

Table A5.1c: SASEC Port Projects in Bangladesh

Project No. BAN-PT-01

Project Name: Chattogram Port Enhancement Project (including Karnaphully Container Terminal at Chattogram Port)

Project Snapshot/Description: Project will expand capacity of Chattogram Port to meet demand and also support subsequent port development projects. Project will integrate those related to SASEC corridors. Chattogram Port will serve as regional gateway port, providing access to SASEC landlocked countries as well as the proximate region.

Estimated Cost ($ million): 200.00

Indicative Funding Source: ADB, other development partners, and Government of Bangladesh

SASEC Road Corr #: 2, 4

Status: Project planned and funding identified, which may or may not be finalized

SASEC OP: OP-3 (ii)

Remarks: ADB is preparing project "SASEC Chittagong Port Enhancement Project Phase I" with proposed ADB financing of $76 million (ADF and OCR).

Project No. BAN-PT-02

Project Name: Upgrading of Chattogram Port: a. New Bay Container Terminal   b. Craneage   c. Laldia Multipurpose/Bulk Terminal

Project Snapshot/Description:
a. Construction of new port outside the River Karnaphuli at Chattogram, to provide new capacity and enable deeper drafted container ships to call.
b. Installation of 10 new gantry cranes for container terminal.
c. Development of terminal mainly for bulk carriers, but some container berths. Being funded on a PPP basis.

Estimated Cost ($ million): 2,772.00

Indicative Funding Source: Chattogram Port Authority, Government of Bangladesh, and Government of India

SASEC Road Corr #: 2, 4

Status: Project planned and funding identified, which may or may not be finalized

SASEC OP: OP-3 (ii)

Remarks: Facility capacity 3.08 million TEU capable of handling containerships up to 5,000 TEU. Will consist of a 1,500-meter multipurpose terminal and a 2,025-meter container terminal with backup facilities and a breakwater. Indian Line of Credit (LOC) $450.00 million.

Project No. BAN-PT-03

Project Name: Patenga Container Terminal

Project Snapshot/Description: Patenga Container Terminal with 3 new jetties. Will be equipped with 2 container cranes to provide handling capacity of 450,000 TEU per year.

Estimated Cost ($ million): 220.00

Indicative Funding Source: Chattogram Port Authority

SASEC Road Corr #: 2, 4

Status: Project completed or under implementation

SASEC OP: OP-3 (ii)

Remarks: Under construction by the Bangladesh Army.

continued next page

Table A5.1c: *Continued*

Project No. BAN-PT-04	Project Name: Matabari Port Project

Project Snapshot/Description: Construction of deepwater commercial port north of Cox's Bazar

Estimated Cost ($ million): 1,500.00

Indicative Funding Source: JICA and Government of Bangladesh

SASEC Road Corr #: 2	SASEC OP: OP-3 (i)

Status: Project planned and funding identified, which may or may not be finalized

Remarks: Loan Agreement for detailed design signed between ERD and JICA.

Project No. BAN-PT-05	Project Name: Development of Mongla Port

Project Snapshot/Description: Construction of Container Terminal (2 jetties), Container Handling Yard, Container Delivery Yard (including modern equipment), Expansion of Port Protected Area with Security System, Construction of Service Vessel Jetty, Port Residential Complex and Community Facilities, Expansion of Bandar Bhaban, Construction of Mechanical Workshop, Marine Workshop Complex with Slipway, Overpass at Digraj Rail Crossing, Procurement of Harbor Crafts (5 nos.), Expansion and Development of Existing Road, Construction of Multi-Level Car Yard.

Estimated Cost ($ million): 714.83

Indicative Funding Source: Government of Bangladesh and Government of India

SASEC Road Corr #: 4	SASEC OP: OP-3 (ii)

Status: Project planned and funding identified, which may or may not be finalized

Remarks: Indian LOC $530.00 million. Part of the spur SASEC Road Corridor 4b.

Project No. BAN-PT-06

Project Name: Development of Payra Port:
- a. **Project on Payra Port's First Terminal and related facilities development**
- b. **Project on Establishment of Payra Port's Multipurpose Terminal**
- c. **Capital and Maintenance Dredging of Rabnabad Channel of Payra Port**
- d. **Development of a Coal/Bulk Terminal at Payra Port**

Project Snapshot/Description:

a. Payra Port`s First Terminal which is a 650 m long Jetty with berthing facilities for two Container Terminals and one General Cargo Terminal. This Project was approved by ECNEC on 4 November 2018.

b. The 1,200 m Multipurpose Terminal has three berths for General Cargo, two for Sand and Aggregates, and one for Grain Terminal under Indian LOC (LOC-3). This Project awaits ECNEC Approval.

c. Under Capital dredging Project Rabnabad Channel will be developed according to PIANC guidelines for safe operation of a 40,000 DWT Bulk Carrier with 10.5 m draft. This PPP Project was approved by CCEA on 5 December 2018.

The coal/bulk terminal has 700-meter jetty with three berths in the first phase to handle 8 million tons of coal per year. The bid document for PPP financing of the project is prepared. After issuance of IFB in early 2019, the Payra Port Authority held a pre-bid meeting with interested bidders in March 2019.

Estimated Cost ($ million): 2,381.00	SASEC Road Corr #: 4
Indicative Funding Source: Government of Bangladesh	SASEC OP: OP-3 (i) and OP-3 (ii)

Status: Project completed or under implementation

Remarks:
- a. First Terminal: $480.47 million–Govt of Bangladesh Financing
- b. Multipurpose Terminal: $615.29 million–Indian LOC-3 Financing
- c. Capital & Maintenance Dredging: $985.30 million–PPP Financing
- d. Coal/Bulk Terminal: $300 million–PPP Financing. Other two jetties with nine berths will be constructed later. This is part of corridor 4c spur road.

ADB = Asian Development Bank, ADF = Asian Development Fund, BAN = Bangladesh, Corr. = Corridor, OCR = ordinary capital resources, OP = operational plan, PPP = public–private partnership, PT = port, SASEC = South Asia Subregional Economic Cooperation, TEU = twenty-foot equivalent unit.

Sources: Asian Development Bank; country submissions in 2018.

Table A5.1d: SASEC Airport Projects in Bangladesh

Project No. BAN-AP-01

Project Name: Third passenger terminal at Hazrat Shahjalal International Airport, Dhaka

Project Snapshot/Description: Construction of 226,000 m² Terminal 3, as well as a 5,900 m² VIP complex, 41,200 m² cargo building, and multilevel car parking building with tunnel. Project also includes construction of several taxiways, a parking apron in Terminal 3, new roads to connect the terminal with the airport road, and a drainage system.

Estimated Cost ($ million): 1,660.00

Indicative Funding Source: Government of Bangladesh and JICA

SASEC Road Corr #: 2, 4

Status: Project completed or under implementation

SASEC OP: OP-5

Remarks: Project is being executed by CAAB and the Ministry of Civil Aviation and Tourism.

Project will more than double the airport's annual passenger handling capacity from the current 8 million to approximately 20 million, and the cargo capacity from 200,000 t to 500,000 t.

Project No. BAN-AP-02

Project Name: Upgrading of Hazrat Shahjalal International Airport, Dhaka:
    a. Airport safety and security system improvement
    b. Expansion and strengthening of cargo apron

Project Snapshot/Description: (a) Upgrades to air safety and security systems in several airports but mainly in Dhaka Airport; (b) Project is to strengthen and widen the existing cargo apron to accommodate more and larger aircraft.

Estimated Cost ($ million): 46.00

Indicative Funding Source: JICA, Government of Bangladesh, and CAAB

SASEC Road Corr #: 2, 4

Status: Project completed or under implementation

SASEC OP: OP-5

Project No. BAN-AP-03

Project Name: Development of Cox's Bazar International Airport

Project Snapshot/Description: Extension and strengthening of runway and taxiway: This will be the first phase of Cox's Bazar Airport development. The area of extension and strengthening will be 197,000 m².

Terminal Building: The building will have an area of 10,912 m²; and the apron and taxiway will measure 49,753 m².

Estimated Cost ($ million): 143.00

Indicative Funding Source: Government of Bangladesh and CAAB

SASEC Road Corr #: 2

Status: Project completed or under implementation

SASEC OP: OP-5

AP = airport, BAN = Bangladesh, CAAB = Civil Aviation Authority of Bangladesh, Corr. = Corridor, JICA = Japan International Cooperation Agency, OP = operational plan, SASEC = South Asia Subregional Economic Cooperation.

Sources: Asian Development Bank; country submissions in 2018.

Table A5.2a: SASEC Road Projects in Bhutan

Project No. BHU-RD-01
Project Name: Construction of Phuentsholing–Chamkuna Road
Project Snapshot/Description: 3.3 km: Construction of southern link feeder road connecting Phuentsholing to Samtse District
Estimated Cost ($ million): 7.00
Indicative Funding Source: Government of Bhutan and ADB
SASEC Road Corr #: 3
Status: Project completed or under implementation
SASEC OP: OP-1 (iii)
Remarks: Covered by SASEC Transport, Trade Facilitation and Logistics Project with ADB funding of $19.61 million (Loan 3421 and Grant 0492). This is part of corridor 3a spur road.
Project No. BHU-RD-02
Project Name: Construction of Pasakha Access Road (PAR)
Project Snapshot/Description: 1.2 km: Construction of access road connecting Pasakha industrial area to new land custom station (LCS) at Allay. Construction of 122.8 meters (m) Bhalujhora bridge, multicellular culvert box, LCS, road work of PAR, and gabion structures.
Estimated Cost ($ million): 7.00
Indicative Funding Source: Government of Bhutan and ADB
SASEC Road Corr #: 3
Status: Project completed or under implementation
SASEC OP: OP-1 (iii)
Remarks: This is part of SASEC Corridor 3a spur road. Covered by SASEC Road Connectivity Project with ADB financing of $50.35 million (Grant 0400 and Loan 3139).
Project No. BHU-RD-03
Project Name: Construction of Northern Bypass Road
Project Snapshot/Description: 2.7 km: Construction of bypass road connecting new mini dry port at Phuentsholing to Thimphu–Phuentsholing Highway
Estimated Cost ($ million): 7.00
Indicative Funding Source: Government of Bhutan and ADB
SASEC Road Corr #: 3
Status: Project completed or under implementation
SASEC OP: OP-1 (iii)
Remarks: Covered by SASEC Road Connectivity Project with ADB financing of $50.35 million (Grant 0400 and Loan 3139). This is part of SASEC Road Corridor 3a spur road.

continued next page

Table A5.2a: *Continued*

Project No. BHU-RD-04
Project Name: Improvement of Rinchending (Kharbandi) to Jumja Road

Project Snapshot/Description: The road, about 55 km under the Department of Roads, is used as an alternative road bypassing Sorchen and Kamji unstable areas. This also forms part of the Southern East–West Highway (SEWH) connecting P'ling–Lhamoizingkha– Sarpang.

Estimated Cost ($ million): 20.00

Indicative Funding Source: Government of Bhutan/TBD

SASEC Road Corr #: 3

Status: Project planned but no funding identified

SASEC OP: OP-1 (iii)

Remarks: This is part of SASEC Road Corridor 3a spur road.

ADB = Asian Development Bank, BHU = Bhutan, Corr. = Corridor, km = kilometer, OP = operational plan, RD = road, SASEC = South Asia Subregional Economic Cooperation, TBD = to be determined.
Sources: Asian Development Bank; country submissions in 2018.

Table A5.2b: SASEC Airport Projects in Bhutan

Project No. BHU-AP-01
Project Name: Upgrading Paro Airport: a. Runway widening, b. Construction of modern cargo terminal

Project Snapshot/Description: (a) The main runway needs widening from 30 m to 45 m to meet international standards for larger aircraft—A319/320; (b) Airport needs dedicated terminal to handle air cargo.

Estimated Cost ($ million): 55.00

Indicative Funding Source: TBD

SASEC Road Corr #: 3

Status: Project planned and funding identified, which may or may not be finalized

SASEC OP: OP-5

Remarks: Possible funding from the Government of India.

Project No. BHU-AP-02
Project Name: Paro Airport: Construction of parallel taxiway and re-modification of departure terminal building

Project Snapshot/Description: Construction of taxiway runway will enable more efficient use of the main runway. Departure terminal needs expansion to cope with concurrent departures.

Estimated Cost ($ million): 2.00

Indicative Funding Source: Government of Bhutan

SASEC Road Corr #: 3

Status: Project completed or under implementation

SASEC OP: OP-5

continued next page

Table A5.2b: *Continued*

Project No. BHU-AP-03
Project Name: Expansion of Gelephu Airport
Project Snapshot/Description: Project requires feasibility and design studies, construction of new 3,000 m runway and associated river diversion, ILS and runway lighting system, apron taxiway, terminal building, hangar, cargo building.
Estimated Cost ($ million): 200.00
Indicative Funding Source: TBD
SASEC Road Corr #: –
Status: Project planned but no funding identified
SASEC OP: OP-5
Remarks: Possible new location for intra-SASEC flights to serve larger aircraft, which would accommodate flight diversions during bad weather at Paro Airport and provide for the transport of supplies during emergencies. Cost includes $20 million for runway.

AP = airport, BHU = Bhutan, Corr. = Corridor, ILS = instrument landing system, m = meter, OP = operational plan, SASEC = South Asia Subregional Economic Cooperation, TBD = to be determined.

Sources: Asian Development Bank; country submissions in 2018.

Table A5.3a: SASEC Road Projects in India

Project No. IND-RD-01
Project Name: Upgrading of Raxaul–Motihari road section
Project Snapshot/Description: NH28A – 67 km: Upgrading from 2-lane to 4-lane, including link road to the new border post
Estimated Cost ($ million): 100.00
Indicative Funding Source: Government of India
SASEC Road Corr #: 1
Status: Project completed or under implementation
SASEC OP: OP-1 (i)

Project No. IND-RD-02
Project Name: Upgrading of Motihari–Pipra Kothi road section
Project Snapshot/Description: NH28 – 15 km: Upgrading from 2-lane to 4-lane extension south of Motihari to link in with 4-lane section southward from Pipra Kothi.
Estimated Cost ($ million): 22.00
Indicative Funding Source: Government of India
SASEC Road Corr #: 1
Status: Project planned but no funding identified
SASEC OP: OP-1 (i)
Remarks: No commitment from NHAI at this stage but could form extension of IND-RD-01.

continued next page

Table A5.3a: *Continued*

Project No. IND-RD-03
Project Name: Upgrading of Muzaffarpur–Patna road section
Project Snapshot/Description: NH77 – 63 km: Upgrading from 2 lanes to 4 lanes
Estimated Cost ($ million): 95.00
Indicative Funding Source: Government of India
SASEC Road Corr #: 1
Status: Project completed or under implementation
SASEC OP: OP-1 (i)

Project No. IND-RD-04
Project Name: Expansion of Patna–Gaya road section
Project Snapshot/Description: NH83 – 105 km: Upgrading from 2 lanes to 4 lanes
Estimated Cost ($ million): 160.00
Indicative Funding Source: Government of India
SASEC Road Corr #: 1
Status: Project completed or under implementation
SASEC OP: OP-1 (i)
Remarks: Recently approved state central road funding of approximately $58.28 million.

Project No. IND-RD-05
Project Name: Widening of Gaya–Dobhi road
Project Snapshot/Description: NH83 – 25 km: Upgrading from 2 lanes to 4 lanes
Estimated Cost ($ million): 38.00
Indicative Funding Source: Government of India
SASEC Road Corr #: 1
Status: Project completed or under implementation
SASEC OP: OP-1 (i)
Remarks: Patna–Dobhi – 127 km 4-laning contract awarded in 2014 ($202.00 million with JICA funding)

Project No. IND-RD-06
Project Name: Widening of Panagarth–Dankuni road section
Project Snapshot/Description: AH1 – 130 km: Possible upgrading from 4 lanes to 6 lanes
Estimated Cost ($ million): 195.00
Indicative Funding Source: Government of India
SASEC Road Corr #: 1
Status: Project completed or under implementation
SASEC OP: OP-1 (i)
Remarks: 4-laning completed.

continued next page

Table A5.3a: *Continued*

Project No. IND-RD-07
Project Name: Development of Road Connections to Diamond Harbor

Project Snapshot/Description: Upgrading of road connections to Diamond Harbor in West Bengal NH-12 (old NH 117) – 123 km

Estimated Cost ($ million): 250.00

Indicative Funding Source: TBD

SASEC Road Corr #: 1

Status: Project planned but no funding identified

SASEC OP: OP-1 (iii)

Remarks: The project has been considered for implementation by NHAI.

Project No. IND-RD-08
Project Name: Upgrading of Madurai Ring Road

Project Snapshot/Description: NH45 – 20 km: Upgrading of Airport–Mattuthavani Ring Road

Estimated Cost ($ million): 30.00

Indicative Funding Source: TBD

SASEC Road Corr #: 2

Status: Project planned but no funding identified

SASEC OP: OP-1 (i)

Remarks: Bypass around Madurai, presently 2 lanes with some construction to 4 lanes.

Project No. IND-RD-09
Project Name: Construction of Elevated Expressway to Chennai Port

Project Snapshot/Description: Elevated expressway would connect port to main north–south highway and ease congestion at the port gate

Estimated Cost ($ million): 225.00

Indicative Funding Source: Government of India

SASEC Road Corr #: 2

Status: Project completed or under implementation

SASEC OP: OP-1 (iii)

Remarks: NHAI has mobilized DPR consultant.

Project No. IND-RD-10
Project Name: Expansion of Chennai-Tada road section

Project Snapshot/Description: AH45 – 43 km: Upgrading to 6 lanes

Estimated Cost ($ million): 60.00

Indicative Funding Source: Government of India

SASEC Road Corr #: 2

Status: Project completed or under implementation

SASEC OP: OP-1 (i)

continued next page

Table A5.3a: *Continued*

Project No. IND-RD-11
Project Name: Expansion of Tada–Nellore road section
Project Snapshot/Description: AH45 – 111 km: Upgrading to 6 lanes
Estimated Cost ($ million): 73.00
Indicative Funding Source: Government of India
SASEC Road Corr #: 2
Status: Project planned and funding identified, which may or may not be finalized
SASEC OP: OP-1 (i)
Project No. IND-RD-12
Project Name: Widening of Bhubaneshwar–Chandikhole road section
Project Snapshot/Description: AH45/NH5 – 61 km to be widened to 6 lanes
Estimated Cost ($ million): 150.00
Indicative Funding Source: Government of India
SASEC Road Corr #: 2
Status: Project completed or under implementation
SASEC OP: OP-1 (i)
Project No. IND-RD-13
Project Name: Upgrading of Paradeep Port–Chandikhole road
Project Snapshot/Description: NH5A – 77 km: feeder road upgrade connecting port with corridor
Estimated Cost ($ million): 115.00
Indicative Funding Source: Government of India
SASEC Road Corr #: 2
Status: Project planned and funding identified, which may or may not be finalized
SASEC OP: OP-1 (iii)
Project No. IND-RD-14
Project Name: Expansion of Chadikhole–Bhadrak road
Project Snapshot/Description: AH45/NH5 – 74 km: Upgrading to 6 lanes
Estimated Cost ($ million): 210.00
Indicative Funding Source: Government of India
SASEC Road Corr #: 2
Status: Project completed or under implementation
SASEC OP: OP-1 (i)

continued next page

Table A5.3a: *Continued*

Project No. IND-RD-15

Project Name: Improvement of Bhadrak–Belasore road

Project Snapshot/Description: AH45/NH5 – 63 km: Partial upgrading from 4 lanes to 6 lanes

Estimated Cost ($ million): 34.00

Indicative Funding Source: Government of India

SASEC Road Corr #: 2

Status: Project completed or under implementation

SASEC OP: OP-1 (i)

Project No. IND-RD-16

Project Name: Improvement of Belasore–Kharagpur road

Project Snapshot/Description: AH45/NH60 – 119 km: Repair of existing 4-lane highway and expansion to 6 lanes

Estimated Cost ($ million): 67.00

Indicative Funding Source: Government of India

SASEC Road Corr #: 2

Status: Project completed or under implementation

SASEC OP: OP-1 (i)

Remarks: NHDP Phase 1 to be executed as BOT (toll) on DBFOT basis.

Project No. IND-RD-17

Project Name: Upgrading of the Belgharia Expressway

Project Snapshot/Description: Various – 8 km: Upgrading of link between Dankuni and NH34 near Barasat into an elevated expressway

Estimated Cost ($ million): 20.00

Indicative Funding Source: TBD

SASEC Road Corr #: 2

Status: Project planned but no funding identified

SASEC OP: OP-1 (i)

Remarks: To be implemented by West Bengal Public Works Department (PWD).

Project No. IND-RD-18

Project Name: Improvement of Barasat–Bangaon road connecting Kolkata to Bangladesh border

Project Snapshot/Description: NH35 – 81 km: Upgrading to 4-lane road link to connect with Petrapole Integrated Check Post

Estimated Cost ($ million): 130.00

Indicative Funding Source: Government of India

SASEC Road Corr #: 2, 3

Status: Project planned and funding identified, which may or may not be finalized

SASEC OP: OP-1 (i)

Remarks: West Bengal PWD is preparing DPR. Implementation of the project will be by West Bengal PWD.

continued next page

Table A5.3a: *Continued*

Project No. IND-RD-19	
Project Name: Upgrading of Barasat–Krishnagar road section	

Project Snapshot/Description: NH34 – 84 km: Upgrading to 4 lanes of main highway north from Kolkata

Estimated Cost ($ million): 124.00

Indicative Funding Source: Government of India

SASEC Road Corr #: 3

Status: Project completed or under implementation

SASEC OP: OP-1 (i)

Remarks: Under NHDP Phase-III on DBFOT (Annuity) Basis

Project No. IND-RD-20	
Project Name: Upgrading of Krishnanagar–Berhampore road	

Project Snapshot/Description: NH34 – 78 km: Upgrading to 4 lanes

Estimated Cost ($ million): 107.00

Indicative Funding Source: Government of India

SASEC Road Corr #: 3

Status: Project completed or under implementation

SASEC OP: OP-1 (i)

Remarks: Under implementation by NHAI.

Project No. IND-RD-21	
Project Name: Upgrading of Berhampore–Farakka road section	

Project Snapshot/Description: NH34 – 94 km: Upgrading to 4 lanes in the State of West Bengal under NHDP Phase-III on DBFOT (Toll) basis

Estimated Cost ($ million): 150.00

Indicative Funding Source: Government of India

SASEC Road Corr #: 3

Status: Project completed or under implementation

SASEC OP: OP-1 (i)

Remarks: Under implementation by NHAI.

Project No. IND-RD-22	
Project Name: Upgrading of Farakka–Raiganj road section	

Project Snapshot/Description: NH34 – 102 km: Upgrading to 4 lanes under NHDP Phase-III on DBFOT (Toll) basis

Estimated Cost ($ million): 154.00

Indicative Funding Source: Government of India

SASEC Road Corr #: 3

Status: Project completed or under implementation

SASEC OP: OP-1 (i)

Remarks: Under implementation by NHAI.

continued next page

Table A5.3a: *Continued*

Project No. IND-RD-23
Project Name: Upgrading of Raiganj–Dalkhola road section
Project Snapshot/Description: NH34 – 54 km: Upgrading to 4 lanes under NHDP Phase-III on DBFOT (Toll) basis
Estimated Cost ($ million): 83.00
Indicative Funding Source: Government of India
SASEC Road Corr #: 3
Status: Project completed or under implementation
SASEC OP: OP-1 (i)
Remarks: Under implementation by NHAI.

Project No. IND-RD-24
Project Name: Expansion of Ghoshpukur–Siliguri road section
Project Snapshot/Description: NH31 – 21 km: Upgrading to 4 lanes
Estimated Cost ($ million): 31.00
Indicative Funding Source: Government of India
SASEC Road Corr #: 3
Status: Project completed or under implementation
SASEC OP: OP-1 (i)
Remarks: Part of East–West Corridor of National Highway Development Project

Project No. IND-RD-25
Project Name: Upgrading of Ghoshpukur–Bipara section
Project Snapshot/Description: NH31 – 131 km: Upgrading to 4 lanes
Estimated Cost ($ million): 200.00
Indicative Funding Source: Government of India
SASEC Road Corr #: 3
Status: Project planned and funding identified, which may or may not be finalized
SASEC OP: OP-1 (i)
Remarks: Part of East–West Corridor of National Highway Development Project

Project No. IND-RD-26
Project Name: Upgrading of Bipara–Salsalabari road section
Project Snapshot/Description: NH31D and NH31C – 70 km: Upgrading to 4 lanes
Estimated Cost ($ million): 105.00
Indicative Funding Source: Government of India
SASEC Road Corr #: 3
Status: Project planned and funding identified, which may or may not be finalized
SASEC OP: OP-1 (i)
Remarks: Part of East–West Corridor of National Highway Development Project

continued next page

Table A5.3a: *Continued*

Project No. IND-RD-27
Project Name: Upgrading of Salsalabari–Bijni section of NH31C

Project Snapshot/Description: NH31C – 100 km: Upgrading to 4 lanes

Estimated Cost ($ million): 150.00

Indicative Funding Source: Government of India

SASEC Road Corr #: 3

Status: Project completed or under implementation

SASEC OP: OP-1 (i)

Remarks: Part of East–West Corridor of National Highway Development Project

Project No. IND-RD-28
Project Name: Upgrading of Bijni–Baihata section NH31C

Project Snapshot/Description: NH31C – 400 km: Upgrading to 4 lanes

Estimated Cost ($ million): 600.00

Indicative Funding Source: Government of India

SASEC Road Corr #: 3

Status: Project completed or under implementation

SASEC OP: OP-1 (i)

Remarks: Part of East–West Corridor of National Highway Development Project

Project No. IND-RD-29
Project Name: Upgrading of Baihata–Guwahati section of NH31C

Project Snapshot/Description: NH31C – 30 km: Upgrading to 4 lanes

Estimated Cost ($ million): 45.00

Indicative Funding Source: Government of India

SASEC Road Corr #: 3

Status: Project completed or under implementation

SASEC OP: OP-1 (i)

Remarks: Part of East–West Corridor of National Highway Development

Project No. IND-RD-30
Project Name: Upgrading of Dabaka–Dimapur road to pass through the edge of the Rengma Hills 2–4 lanes

Project Snapshot/Description: AH1 – 110 km: Upgrading to 4 lanes in some sections and upgrading to 2 lanes in hilly stretches

Estimated Cost ($ million): 165.00

Indicative Funding Source: Government of India

SASEC Road Corr #: 3

Status: Project completed or under implementation

SASEC OP: OP-1 (i)

continued next page

Table A5.3a: *Continued*

Project No. IND-RD-31
Project Name: Upgrading of Dimapur–Kohima
Project Snapshot/Description: NH39 – 15 km: 4-laning of Dimapur–Kohima section km 124–km 139
Estimated Cost ($ million): 55.00
Indicative Funding Source: Government of India
SASEC Road Corr #: 3
Status: Project completed or under implementation
SASEC OP: OP-1 (i)

Project No. IND-RD-32
Project Name: Upgrading of Dimapur–Kohima
Project Snapshot/Description: NH39 – 14 km: 4-laning of Dimapur–Kohima section
Estimated Cost ($ million): 49.00
Indicative Funding Source: Government of India
SASEC Road Corr #: 3
Status: Project completed or under implementation
SASEC OP: OP-1 (i)

Project No. IND-RD-33
Project Name: Upgrading of Dimapur–Kohima
Project Snapshot/Description: NH39 – 14 km: 4-laning of Dimapur–Kohima
Estimated Cost ($ million): 49.00
Indicative Funding Source: Government of India
SASEC Road Corr #: 3
Status: Project completed or under implementation
SASEC OP: OP-1 (i)

Project No. IND-RD-34
Project Name: Assam–Nagaland connectivity 1
Project Snapshot/Description: NH 36/39 – 20 km: Construction of 4–6-lanes of the Daboka Dimapur section–Dimapur Bypass
Estimated Cost ($ million): 55.00
Indicative Funding Source: Government of India
SASEC Road Corr #: 3
Status: Project completed or under implementation
SASEC OP: OP-1 (i)

continued next page

Table A5.3a: *Continued*

Project No. IND-RD-35
Project Name: Assam–Nagaland connectivity 2

Project Snapshot/Description: NH 36/39 – 14 km: Construction of Dimapur Bypass (Assam Portion) with 4–6 lane pavement on EPC basis up to end point of the Assam portion

Estimated Cost ($ million): 56.00

Indicative Funding Source: Government of India

SASEC Road Corr #: 3

Status: Project planned and funding identified, which may or may not be finalized

SASEC OP: OP-1 (i)

Project No. IND-RD-36
Project Name: Improvement to Kohima–Mao road section

Project Snapshot/Description: NH 39 – 36 km: Upgrading to connect Kohima in Nagaland to Manipur Part 1

Estimated Cost ($ million): 64.00

Indicative Funding Source: ADB

SASEC Road Corr #: 3

Status: Project planned and funding identified, which may or may not be finalized

SASEC OP: OP-1 (i)

Remarks: DPR finalized. Included in ADB pipeline.

Project No. IND-RD-37
Project Name: Improvement to Mao–Imphal road section

Project Snapshot/Description: NH 39 – 106 km: Upgrading to connect Kohima in Nagaland to Manipur

Estimated Cost ($ million): 189.00

Indicative Funding Source: ADB

SASEC Road Corr #: 3

Status: Project planned and funding identified, which may or may not be finalized

SASEC OP: OP-1 (i)

Remarks: DPR finalized. Construction planned in 2021–2022.

Project No. IND-RD-38
Project Name: Improvement of Imphal–Moreh road

Project Snapshot/Description: NH39 – 55 km and 20 km: Upgrade to two road sections in two packages

Estimated Cost ($ million): 135.00

Indicative Funding Source: ADB

SASEC Road Corr #: 3

Status: Project completed or under implementation

SASEC OP: OP-1 (ii)

Remarks: Covered by the ADB project SASEC Road Connectivity Investment Program–Tranche II with ADB financing of $150 million (Loan 3690). Loan agreement was signed in October 2018. This tranche II of an ADB MFF will finance two packages.

continued next page

Table A5.3a: *Continued*

Project No. IND-RD-39
Project Name: **Construction of Moreh Bypass**

Project Snapshot/Description: 3 km of road link to bypass Moreh town and to connect to Integrated Check Post on India–Myanmar border

Estimated Cost ($ million): 1.00

Indicative Funding Source: Government of India

SASEC Road Corr #: 3

Status: Project planned and funding identified, which may or may not be finalized

SASEC OP: OP-1 (ii)

Remarks: Alignment finalized.

Project No. IND-RD-40
Project Name: **Upgrading of Jaigaon/Pasakha border–Changrabandha border link road**

Project Snapshot/Description: AH48 – 90 km: Upgrading to 2–4 lanes

Estimated Cost ($ million): 89.00

Indicative Funding Source: ADB and Government of India

SASEC Road Corr #: 4

Status: Project completed or under implementation

SASEC OP: OP-1 (i), OP-1 (ii)

Project No. IND-RD-41
Project Name: **Construction of link road to Pasakha ICD**

Project Snapshot/Description: 5 km: Construction of new link road to Pasakha ICD in Bhutan

Estimated Cost ($ million): 10.00

Indicative Funding Source: Government of India

SASEC Road Corr #: 3

Status: project completed or under implementation

SASEC OP: OP-1 (ii)

Remarks: Being implemented by NHIDCL. This is part of SASEC Road Corridor 3a spur road.

Project No. IND-RD-42
Project Name: **Mechi Bridge on India–Nepal border**

Project Snapshot/Description: AH2 – 1.6 km: Mechi Bridge and approaches on India–Nepal border linking Kakarvitta and Panitanki

Estimated Cost ($ million): 16.00

Indicative Funding Source: ADB and Government of India

SASEC Road Corr #: 4

Status: Project completed or under implementation

SASEC OP: OP-1 (i)

Remarks: Covered by the ADB project SASEC Road Connectivity Investment Program–Tranche II with ADB financing of $150 million (Loan 3690). Loan agreement signed in October 2018. Being implemented by NHIDCL.

continued next page

Table A5.3a: *Continued*

Project No. **IND-RD-43**
Project Name: **Upgrading of Panitanki–Fulbari border link roads**

Project Snapshot/Description: AH2 – 37 km: 4-laning of connecting road between Nepal and Bangladesh

Estimated Cost ($ million): 63.00

Indicative Funding Source: ADB and Government of India

SASEC Road Corr #: 4

Status: Project completed or under implementation

SASEC OP: OP-1 (i)

Project No. **IND-RD-44**
Project Name: **Upgrading of Dawki to Shillong road including rehabilitation of Dawki bridge at border**

Project Snapshot/Description: NH 40 – 95 km: road upgrade and suspension bridge rehabilitation project; included in Bharatmala Program

Estimated Cost ($ million): 186.00

Indicative Funding Source: JICA and Government of India

SASEC Road Corr #: 5

Status: Project planned and funding identified, which may or may not be finalized

SASEC OP: OP-1 (ii)

Remarks: Final DPR submitted in August 2017. JICA loan agreement signed in March 2018.

Project No. **IND-RD-45**
Project Name: **Upgrading of Hasimara–Jaigaon road section**

Project Snapshot/Description: AH48 – 17 km: Upgrading to 2–4 lanes

Estimated Cost ($ million): 25.00

Indicative Funding Source: Government of India and ADB

SASEC Road Corr #: 3

Status: Project completed or under implementation

SASEC OP: OP-1 (ii)

Remarks: Under construction as part of project linking Bhutan with Bangladesh border. This is part of SASEC Road Corridor 3a spur road.

ADB = Asian Development Bank, AH = Asian Highway, BOT = build–operate–transfer, Corr. = Corridor, DBFOT = design–build–finance–operate–transfer, DPR = detailed project report, ICD = inland container depot, IND = India, JICA = Japan International Cooperation Agency, km = kilometer, NH = national highway, NHAI = National Highways Authority of India, NHDP = National Highways Development Project, NHIDCL = National Highways and Infrastructure Development Corporation, OP = operational plan, PWD = Public Works Department, RD = road, SASEC = South Asia Subregional Economic Cooperation, TBD = to be determined.

Sources: Asian Development Bank; country submissions in 2018.

Table A5.3b: SASEC Railway Projects in India

Project No. IND-RW-01
Project Name: New railway link Akhaura–Agartala
Project Snapshot/Description: 5 km: To serve as important cross-border connection into northeastern states of India
Estimated Cost ($ million): 50
Indicative Funding Source: Government of India
SASEC Road Corr #: 2
Status: Project completed or under implementation
SASEC OP: OP-2 (i)
Remarks: This is part of SASEC Road Corridor 2a spur road.

Corr. = Corridor, IND = India, km = kilometer, OP = operational plan, RW = railway, SASEC = South Asia Subregional Economic Cooperation.
Sources: Asian Development Bank; country submissions in 2018.

Table A5.3c: SASEC Port Projects in India

Project No. IND-PT-01
Project Name: Expansion of Inner Harbour at Paradip Port
Project Snapshot/Description: Expansion of Inner Harbor at Paradip Port
Estimated Cost ($ million): 226.00
Indicative Funding Source: Government of India
SASEC Road Corr #: 2
Status: Project planned and funding identified, which may or may not finalized
SASEC OP: OP-3 (ii)
Remarks: DPR has been prepared.
Project No. IND-PT-02
Project Name: Development of Outer Harbor nearer to south of South Breakwater at Paradip Port
Project Snapshot/Description: Development of Outer Harbor nearer to south of South Breakwater at Paradip Port
Estimated Cost ($ million): 2,454.00
Indicative Funding Source: Government of India
SASEC Road Corr #: 2
Status: Project planned and funding identified, which may or may not finalized
SASEC OP: OP-3 (ii)

continued next page

Table A5.3c: *Continued*

Project No. IND-PT-03

Project Name: Haldia Port Upgrading: a. Augmentation of Capacity of Dock Complex b. Construction of 3 new berths

Project Snapshot/Description: a. Augmentation of capacity of Haldia Dock Complex, by way of new lock gate in existing dock/basin and modification of existing lock gate;
b. Provision of 2 liquid cargo and 1 dry-bulk facility to augment capacity

Estimated Cost ($ million): 295.00

Indicative Funding Source: KPT

SASEC Road Corr #: 2

Status: Project planned and funding identified, which may or may not finalized

SASEC OP: OP-3 (ii)

Remarks: One liquid-cargo terminal (2 million tons), primarily for edible oil, at Salukhali, 15 km north of Haldia; two outer terminals—one for dry-bulk cargo (5 million tons) and another liquid-cargo terminal (2 million tons) also proposed.

Project No. IND-PT-04

Project Name: V.O. Chidambaranagar Port Trust, Thoothukudi

Project Snapshot/Description: Deepening Harbor Basin and Approach Channel, Construction of Breakwater/Bubble Protection Bund, Strengthening Berths 1–6, Widening of Port Entrance Channel

Estimated Cost ($ million): 462.00

Indicative Funding Source: ADB and Government of India

SASEC Road Corr #: 2

Status: Project planned and funding identified, which may or may not finalized

SASEC OP: OP-3 (i)

Remarks: Project will enable the port to handle demands of being a major power hub in southern Tamil Nadu, as well as growth of several industries.

The "Tuticorin Port Expansion Project" is being prepared to augment the port's capacity through an Inner Harbour Development Program (to be considered for ADB financing).

ADB = Asian Development Bank, Corr. = Corridor, IND = India, km = kilometer, OP = operational plan, PT = port, SASEC = South Asia Subregional Economic Cooperation.

Sources: Asian Development Bank; country submissions in 2018.

Table A5.3d: SASEC Airport Projects in India

Project No. IND-AP-01

Project Name: Chennai Airport Expansion Program

Project Snapshot/Description: The program includes construction of a new domestic terminal and expansion of the current international terminal, other terminal buildings, parking garage structures, and the roadway access system

Estimated Cost ($ million): 335.00

Indicative Funding Source: Airports Authority of India and Government of India

SASEC Road Corr #: 2

Status: Project completed or under implementation   **SASEC OP:** OP-5

Project No. IND-AP-02

Project Name: Guwahati Airport

Project Snapshot/Description: Construction of a new passenger terminal with a capacity to handle 9 million passengers per year.

Estimated Cost ($ million): 186.00

Indicative Funding Source: Government of India

SASEC Road Corr #: 2

Status: Project completed or under implementation   **SASEC OP:** OP-5

AP = airport, Corr. = Corridor, IND = India, OP = operational plan, SASEC = South Asia Subregional Economic Cooperation.
Sources: Asian Development Bank; country submissions in 2018.

Table A5.4a: SASEC Road Projects in Myanmar

Project No. MYA-RD-01

Project Name: Rehabilitation of Tamu–Kyigone–Kalewa (TKK) Road

Project Snapshot/Description: Trilateral Highway – 150 km: Built in 2009 now requires provision of 69 new bridges

Estimated Cost ($ million): 143.00

Indicative Funding Source: Government of India and Government of Myanmar

SASEC Road Corr #: 3

Status: Project completed or under implementation   **SASEC OP:** OP-1 (ii)

Remarks: Being implemented by NHAI of India.

Project No. MYA-RD-02

Project Name: Construction of Kalewa–Yargi Road

Project Snapshot/Description: 120 km: Upgrading to 2-lane highway

Estimated Cost ($ million): 190.00

Indicative Funding Source: Government of India and Government of Myanmar

SASEC Road Corr #: 3

Status: Project completed or under implementation   **SASEC OP:** OP-1 (ii)

Remarks: Being implemented by NHAI of India. MOU signed in August 2016. Contract for construction signed in April 2018.

continued next page

Table A5.4a: *Continued*

Project No. MYA-RD-03	
Project Name: Upgrading of Mandalay–Bago road	
Project Snapshot/Description: NH1 – 518 km: Widening of 2-lane road	
Estimated Cost ($ million): 500.00	
Indicative Funding Source: BOT basis	
SASEC Road Corr #: 3	
Status: Project completed or under implementation	**SASEC OP:** OP-1 (i)

Project No. MYA-RD-04	
Project Name: Safety improvement on Yangon–Mandalay Expressway	
Project Snapshot/Description: 64 km of expressway improvement (Yangon–Bago) and about 530 km of safety improvements	
Estimated Cost ($ million): 91.00	
Indicative Funding Source: Government of Myanmar	
SASEC Road Corr #: 3	
Status: Project planned and funding identified, may or may not be finalized	**SASEC OP:** OP-1 (i)

Project No. MYA-RD-05	
Project Name: Construction of new bridge across Bago River	
Project Snapshot/Description: NH2 – 1 km: Construction of new bridge on NH2 to improve access to Thilawa	
Estimated Cost ($ million): 289.00	
Indicative Funding Source: Government of Myanmar and JICA	
SASEC Road Corr #: 3	
Status: Project planned and funding identified, may or may not be finalized	**SASEC OP:** OP-1 (i)

Project No. MYA-RD-06	
Project Name: Bago Bypass Project	
Project Snapshot/Description: NH2 – Elimination of bottleneck along main north–south route	
Estimated Cost ($ million): 25.00	
Indicative Funding Source: Government of Myanmar	
SASEC Road Corr #: 3	
Status: Project planned and funding identified, may or may not be finalized	**SASEC OP:** OP-1 (i)

Project No. MYA-RD-07	
Project Name: Upgrade of BagoThilawa road	
Project Snapshot/Description: 99 km section upgrading to 2-lane highway	
Estimated Cost ($ million): 104.00	
Indicative Funding Source: Government of Myanmar	
SASEC Road Corr #: 3	
Status: Project planned and funding identified, may or may not be finalized	**SASEC OP:** OP-1 (ii)
Remarks: Improved access to port and Special Economic Zone	

continued next page

Table A5.4a: *Continued*

Project No. MYA-RD-08

Project Name: Thilawa–East Dagon Road Project

Project Snapshot/Description: Construction of 33 km, 4-lane road connecting East Dagon with Thilawa port

The components of the project include (i) the reconstruction of 5.5 km of the currently partially improved 4-lane divided road; (ii) widening of 16.5 km of a recently constructed 2-lane road into a 4-lane divided typical section, along with the construction of additional 2-lane bridges; (iii) resurfacing and minor repairs of the 1.4 km Thanlyin Bridge, including a verification of the original bridge design and as-built drawings, and a complete detailed bridge-condition survey; and (iv) the reconstruction and widening of a northerly 9.4 km section of the 2-lane road connection with Highway No. 2.

Estimated Cost ($ million): 42.00

Indicative Funding Source: TBD

SASEC Road Corr #: 3

Status: Project planned but no funding identified   **SASEC OP:** OP-1 (i)

Project No. MYA-RD-09

Project Name: Upgrading of Thaton–Eindu Road

Project Snapshot/Description: AH1 – 68 km: Upgrading to 2-lane highway

Estimated Cost ($ million): 51.00

Indicative Funding Source: Government of Thailand and Government of Myanmar

SASEC Road Corr #: 3

Status: Project planned and funding identified, may or may not be finalized   **SASEC OP:** OP-1 (ii)

Remarks: Agreement signed between governments of Myanmar and Thailand in February 2017

Project No. MYA-RD-10

Project Name: Upgrading of Eindu-Kawkareik section

Project Snapshot/Description: AH1– 66 km: Upgrading of 2-lane section near Thai Border

Estimated Cost ($ million): 122.00

Indicative Funding Source: ADB and Government of Myanmar

SASEC Road Corr #: 3

Status: Project completed or under implementation   **SASEC OP:** OP-1 (ii)

AH = Asian Highway, BOT = build–operate–transfer, Corr. = Corridor, JICA = Japan International Cooperation Agency, km = kilometer, MOU = memorandum of understanding, MYA = Myanmar, NH = national highway, NHAI = National Highways Authority of India, OP = operational plan, RD = road, TBD = to be determined, SASEC = South Asia Subregional Economic Cooperation.

Sources: Asian Development Bank; country submissions in 2018.

Table A5.4b: SASEC Airport Projects in Myanmar

Project No. MYA-AP-01
Project Name: Renovation of Terminal 2 (T2) at Yangon International Airport

Project Snapshot/Description: Program to renovate and upgrade the existing Terminal 2 infrastructure

Estimated Cost ($ million): 666.00

Indicative Funding Source: Government of Myanmar

SASEC Road Corr #: 2

Status: Project completed or under implementation

SASEC OP: OP-5

Project No. MYA-AP-02
Project Name: Hanthawaddy International Airport

Project Snapshot/Description: Construction of greenfield airport. The new airport is designed to accommodate 12 million passengers after completion of phase 1, with capacity to expand to 20 million after phase 2, and capacity of 30 million once fully completed. To be built on more than 3,600 hectares of land in Bago, 80 km from Yangon, the airport is intended to ease congestion at Yangon International Airport.

Estimated Cost ($ million): 1,812.00

Indicative Funding Source: Japan ODA

SASEC Road Corr #: 2

Status: Project planned and funding identified, which may or may not be finalized

SASEC OP: OP-5

Project No. MYA-AP-03
Project Name: Development of new cargo terminal at Mandalay International Airport

Project Snapshot/Description: Accommodation of high-density, scheduled international flights at an airport in central Myanmar, establishing a direct air route and new aviation cargo hub, linking Europe and points in Asia

Estimated Cost ($ million): 5.00

Indicative Funding Source: Private

SASEC Road Corr #: 2

Status: Project completed or under implementation

SASEC OP: OP-5

AP = airport, Corr. = Corridor, km = kilometer, MYA = Myanmar, ODA = official development assistance, OP = operational plan, SASEC = South Asia Subregional Economic Cooperation.

Sources: Asian Development Bank; country submissions in 2018.

Table A5.5a: SASEC Road Projects in Nepal

Project No. NEP-RD-01

Project Name: Upgrading of Kathmandu–Naubise–Mugling road

Project Snapshot/Description: AH42 – 96 km: Subcomponent of the Nepal–India Regional Trade and Transport Project (NIRTTP) involving the improvement of existing 96 km into a dedicated 2-lane road with full application of road safety measures, bypasses, and 2-lane new road on the other bank of the Trishuli River.

Estimated Cost ($ million): 257.00

Indicative Funding Source: World Bank and Government of Nepal

SASEC Road Corr #: 1, 4

Status: Project planned and funding identified, which may or may not be finalized   **SASEC OP:** OP-1 (ii)

Remarks: NIRTTP is being implemented by the Government of Nepal with assistance from the World Bank. NIRTTP was approved in 2013. It is being implemented by three different ministries. A subcomponent of NIRTTP project is to prepare a feasibility study of Kathmandu (Nagdhunga)–Naubise–Mugling road improvement.

Project No. NEP-RD-02

Project Name: Upgrading of Mugling–Narayanghat highway

Project Snapshot/Description: AH-42 – 35 km: Improvement and widening of Mugling–Narayanghat Highway

Estimated Cost ($ million): 310.00

Indicative Funding Source: World Bank and Government of Nepal

SASEC Road Corr #: 1, 4

Status: Project completed or under implementation   **SASEC OP:** OP-1 (ii)

Project No. NEP-RD-03

Project Name: Upgrading of Pathlaiya–Hetauda–Narayanghat road

Project Snapshot/Description: AH-2 – Upgrading of road to 4 lanes: Pathlaiya–Hetauda–Narayanghat road (106 km)

Estimated Cost ($ million): 220.00

Indicative Funding Source: ADB and Government of Nepal

SASEC Road Corr #: 1, 4

Status: Project planned and funding identified, which may or may not be finalized   **SASEC OP:** OP-1 (i)

Remarks: Project included in ADB's indicative assistance pipeline for 2021/2022 as SASEC Highway Enhancement Project I and II.

Project No. NEP-RD-04

Project Name: Construction of a new 4-lane expressway from Kathmandu to Nijgadh

Project Snapshot/Description: 76 km: "Fast Track Road" (from Kathmandu to Nijgadh) is designed to provide shorter and safer access from Kathmandu to the southern Terai region to the south and to the Indian border at Birgunj.

Estimated Cost ($ million): 1,200.00

Indicative Funding Source: Government of Nepal

SASEC Road Corr #: 1

Status: Project planned and funding identified, which may or may not be finalized   **SASEC OP:** OP-1 (i)

Remarks: Complementary alternate route to SASEC Road Corridor 1 and 4 in Nepal. This is part of SASEC Road Corridor 1a spur road.

continued next page

Table A5.5a: *Continued*

Project No. NEP-RD-05
Project Name: Upgrading of Pathlaiya–Birgunj road
Project Snapshot/Description: AH-42 – 29 km: Upgrade of main road to the border (Tribuvan Highway) at Birgunj, including link road to the new border crossing facility
Estimated Cost ($ million): 30.00
Indicative Funding Source: Government of Nepal
SASEC Road Corr #: 1
Status: Project completed or under implementation
SASEC OP: OP-1 (i)

Project No. NEP-RD-06
Project Name: Upgrading of Dhalkebar–Pathlaiya section
Project Snapshot/Description: AH-2 – 92 km: Expansion of road section of East–West Highway between Dhalkebar and Pathlaiya to 4 lanes
Estimated Cost ($ million): 200.00
Indicative Funding Source: World Bank and Government of Nepal
SASEC Road Corr #: 4
Status: Project completed or under implementation
SASEC OP: OP-1 (i)
Remarks: Construction of bridges ongoing under World Bank support.

Project No. NEP-RD-07
Project Name: Upgrading of Dhalkebar section
Project Snapshot/Description: AH-2 – 20.6 km: Upgrading of road to 4 lanes
Estimated Cost ($ million): 50.00
Indicative Funding Source: ADB and Government of Nepal
SASEC Road Corr #: 4
Status: Project planned and funding identified, which may or may not be finalized
SASEC OP: OP-1 (i)
Remarks: Project included in ADB's indicative assistance pipeline for 2021/2022 as SASEC Highway Enhancement Project I and II.

continued next page

Table A5.5a: *Continued*

Project No. NEP-RD-08
Project Name: Upgrading of Kamala section

Project Snapshot/Description: AH-2 – 87 km: Upgrading of road to 4 lanes

Estimated Cost ($ million): 180.00

Indicative Funding Source: ADB and Government of Nepal

SASEC Road Corr #: 4

Status: Project completed or under implementation

SASEC OP: OP-1 (i)

Remarks: Covered by the ADB project SASEC Highway Improvement Project with ADB funding of $180 million (Loan 3722) approved by ADB in 2018.

Project No. NEP-RD-09
Project Name: Upgrading of Kakarvitta–Laukahi section

Project Snapshot/Description: AH-2 – 120 km: Upgrading of road to 4 lanes between Kakarvitta and Laukahi at the eastern end of the East–West Highway

Estimated Cost ($ million): 250.00

Indicative Funding Source: ADB and Government of Nepal

SASEC Road Corr #: 4

Status: Project planned and funding identified, which may or may not be finalized

SASEC OP: OP-1 (i)

Remarks: Project included in ADB's indicative assistance pipeline for 2021–2022 as SASEC Highway Enhancement Project I and II.

Project No. NEP-RD-10
Project Name: Upgrading of national highway between Mugling and Pokhara

Project Snapshot/Description: To upgrade to 4 lanes the 90 km section between Mugling and Pokhara to AH Class 1 standard. Includes financing two major bridges along Seti and Madi rivers. Mugling is a major junction and connects to Narayanghat and onward to India.

Estimated Cost ($ million): 175.00

Indicative Funding Source: ADB and Government of Nepal

SASEC Road Corr #: 4

Status: Project planned and funding identified, which may or may not be finalized

SASEC OP: OP-1 (i)

Remarks: Project included in ADB's indicative assistance pipeline for 2019 as SASEC Mugling–Pokhara Highway Improvement Project Phase I with ADB loan of $241.00 million.

ADB = Asian Development Bank, AH = Asian Highway, Corr. = Corridor, km = kilometer, NEP = Nepal, OP = operational plan, RD = road, SASEC = South Asia Subregional Economic Cooperation.

Sources: Asian Development Bank; country submissions in 2018.

Table A5.5b: SASEC Airport Projects in Nepal

Project No. NEP-AP-01
Project Name: Tribhuvan International Airport Capacity Expansion Investment Program
Project Snapshot/Description: Enhancement of facilities at the country's major international airport including, airside facilities, runways, taxiways, aprons, and communication navigation surveillance equipment
Estimated Cost ($ million): 220.00
Indicative Funding Source: ADB and Government of Nepal
SASEC Road Corr #: 1
Status: Project planned and funding identified, may or may not be finalized
SASEC OP: OP-5
Remarks: DPR supported by ADB. Included in ADB's indicative pipeline for 2020 as Tribhuvan International Airport Capacity Expansion Investment Program (Tranche 1) with proposed ADB financing of $105 million.
Project No. NEP-AP-02
Project Name: Expansion and upgrading of Gautam Buddha Airport, about 280 km west of Kathmandu
Project Snapshot/Description: Upgrading of the facility to an international airport (Category E as per ICAO guidelines)
Estimated Cost ($ million): 65.00
Indicative Funding Source: ADB, OPEC, Government of Nepal
SASEC Road Corr #: 1
Status: Project completed or under implementation
SASEC OP: OP-5
Remarks: Part of the South Asia Tourism Infrastructure Development Project (Bangladesh, India, and Nepal). ADB financing for Nepal amounts to $25.5 million (Grant 0179 and Loan 2579); OPEC Fund for International Development financing amounts to $15 million (Loan 8247). Additional financing for the entire project amounts to $33 million (Grant 0383 and Loan 3117).

ADB = Asian Development Bank, AP = airport, Corr. = Corridor, DPR = detailed project report, NEP = Nepal, OP = operational plan, SASEC = South Asia Subregional Economic Cooperation.

Sources: Asian Development Bank; country submissions in 2018.

Table A5.6a: SASEC Road Projects in Sri Lanka

Project No. SL-RD-01

Project Name: Construction of Central Expressway

Project Snapshot/Description: 37 km: Stage 1 – Construction of expressway from Kadawatha to Meerigama

Estimated Cost ($ million): 1,000

Indicative Funding Source: The PRC and Government of Sri Lanka

SASEC Road Corr #: 6

Status: Project planned and funding identified, which may or may not be finalized

SASEC OP: OP-1 (i)

Remarks: FS and Design completed. Funding agreed with Export–Import Bank of China.

Project No. SL-RD-02

Project Name: Construction of Central Expressway

Project Snapshot/Description: 49 km: Stage II – Construction of expressway Meerigama to Kurunegala and Ambepussa link road

Estimated Cost ($ million): 952

Indicative Funding Source: The PRC and Government of Sri Lanka

SASEC Road Corr #: 6

Status: Project completed or under implementation

SASEC OP: OP-1 (i)

Remarks: FS completed. Construction to be completed in 2019.

Project No. SL-RD-03

Project Name: Construction of Central Expressway

Project Snapshot/Description: 33 km: Stage III – Construction of Pothuhera to Galagedara (Kandy) section

Estimated Cost ($ million): 500

Indicative Funding Source: The PRC and Government of Sri Lanka

SASEC Road Corr #: 6

Status: Project planned and funding identified, which may or may not be finalized

SASEC OP: OP-1 (i)

Remarks: FS completed. This is part of SASEC Road Corridor 6a spur road.

Project No. SL-RD-04

Project Name: Construction of Central Expressway

Project Snapshot/Description: 62 km: Stage IV – Construction of the Kurunegala to Dambulla section

Estimated Cost ($ million): 1,000.00

Indicative Funding Source: The PRC and Government of Sri Lanka

SASEC Road Corr #: 6

Status: Project planned and funding identified, which may or may not be finalized

SASEC OP: OP-1 (i)

Remarks: FS completed.

continued next page

Table A5.6a: *Continued*

Project No. SL-RD-05
Project Name: Development of road sections from Dambulla to Trincomalee
Project Snapshot/Description: A12 – 101 km: Construction of 4-lane road as an extension of the Central Expressway
Estimated Cost ($ million): 540.00
Indicative Funding Source: Government of Sri Lanka and Government of India
SASEC Road Corr #: 6
Status: Project planned and funding identified, which may or may not be finalized
SASEC OP: OP-1 (i)
Remarks: MOU signed with India includes development of Dambulla–Trincomalee road as an Expressway through joint investments by India and Sri Lanka.

Project No. SL-RD-06
Project Name: Construction of city links to Colombo Port
Project Snapshot/Description: 17 km: Widening of the Kelani Bridge to 6 lanes and new elevated extension to Colombo port
Estimated Cost ($ million): 100.00
Indicative Funding Source: JICA and Government of Sri Lanka
SASEC Road Corr #: 6
Status: Project completed or under implementation
SASEC OP: OP-1 (iii)

Project No. SL-RD-07
Project Name: Elevated toll highway between the New Kelani Bridge (NKB) and port gate
Project Snapshot/Description: 5.3 km: Proposed project for construction of elevated highway between the NKB, Galle Face and the port. It will link the port with the Colombo–Katunayake Expressway via the NKB, and then extend the expressway network into the city.
Estimated Cost ($ million): 593.00
Indicative Funding Source: ADB and Government of Sri Lanka
SASEC Road Corr #: 6
Status: Project completed or under implementation
SASEC OP: OP-1 (iii)
Remarks: ADB approved, in October 2018, the SASEC Port Access Elevated Highway Project. ADB financing of $300 million was committed in January 2019 (Loan 3716).
A $1.25 million TA project funded by JFPR is piggybacked to provide support for improving Sri Lanka's trade logistics and optimize benefits from improved connectivity to the port.

ADB = Asian Development Bank, FS = feasibility study, JICA = Japan International Cooperation Agency, km = kilometer, MOU = memorandum of understanding, OP = operational plan, PRC = People's Republic of China, RD = road, SASEC = South Asia Subregional Economic Cooperation, SL = Sri Lanka, TA = technical assistance.

Sources: Asian Development Bank; country submissions in 2018.

Table A5.6b: SASEC Port Projects in Sri Lanka

Project No. SL-PT-01
Project Name: Completion and Equipping of Eastern Terminal

Project Snapshot/Description: Development of the eastern terminal to be able to process 2.4 million TEU per year

Estimated Cost ($ million): 430.00

Indicative Funding Source: TBD	**SASEC Road Corr #:** 6
Status: Project planned but no funding identified	**SASEC OP:** OP-3 (ii)

Project No. SL-PT-02
Project Name: Construction of Western Terminal

Project Snapshot/Description: Construction of similar facility to complement southern and eastern terminals to enable port to handle over 7 million TEU in outer harbor

Estimated Cost ($ million): 600.00

Indicative Funding Source: TBD	**SASEC Road Corr #:** 6
Status: Project planned but no funding identified	**SASEC OP:** OP-3 (ii)

Project No. SL-PT-03
Project Name: SASEC Port and Logistics Development Project

Project Snapshot/Description: The project will enhance commercial operations of ports by the Sri Lanka Port Authority. More specifically, the project will (i) meet the multimodal transport demands of the country's imports and exports, (ii) expand capacity of the ports serving specific parts of the country, and (iii) enable the rehabilitation of port facilities and consider future port expansion.

The project will develop port and logistics infrastructure in accordance with the National Port Master Plan.

Estimated Cost ($ million): 200.00

Indicative Funding Source: ADB	**SASEC Road Corr #:** 6
Status: Project planned and funding identified, which may or may not be finalized	**SASEC OP:** OP-3 (ii)

ADB = Asian Development Bank, OP = operational plan, PT = port, RD = road, SASEC = South Asia Subregional Economic Cooperation, SL = Sri Lanka, TBD = to be determined, TEU = twenty-foot equivalent unit.
Sources: Asian Development Bank; country submissions in 2018.

Table A5.6c: SASEC Airport Projects in Sri Lanka

Project No. SL-AP-01
Project Name: Bandaranaike International Airport Development Phase II Stage II

Project Snapshot/Description: Phase II Stage II of the development program consists of construction of a new multilevel terminal building, Pier nos. 2 and 3 with a linked concourse, a new parking apron and connecting taxiways, elevated access roads, a multistory carpark, and other public utilities.

Project is to increase the passenger handling capacity by an additional 9 million passengers per year and to improve passenger convenience.

Estimated Cost ($ million): 550.00

Indicative Funding Source: JICA and Government of Sri Lanka

Status: Project completed or under implementation	**SASEC OP:** OP-5

AP = airport, JICA = Japan International Cooperation Agency, OP = operational plan, SASEC = South Asia Subregional Economic Cooperation, SL = Sri Lanka.
Sources: Asian Development Bank; country submissions in 2018.

APPENDIX 6

SASEC TRADE FACILITATION PROJECTS – BY COUNTRY

Table A6.1: SASEC Trade Facilitation Projects in Bangladesh

Project No. BAN-TF-01

Project Name: Development of infrastructure at land customs stations (LCS)

Project Snapshot/Description: Refurbishment and/or rehabilitation of border crossing points by developing facilities and connectivity, for enhanced efficiency on cross-border trade and transport.

Project will include

i. Develop and infrastructural facilities and connectivity links appropriate to each LCS, to bridge the gaps;
ii. Procurement of scanners;
iii. Automation of operations;
iv. Establishing a central customs laboratory in Dhaka; and
v. Capacity building and suitable institutional arrangements for cross-border coordination of the development of the facilities

Estimated Cost ($ million): 150.00

Indicative Funding Source: ADB

SASEC OP: 5

Status: Project planned and funding identified, which may or may not be finalized

Project No. BAN-TF-02

Project Name: Development of Inland Container Depot (ICD) in Tongi and Joydevpur

Project Snapshot/Description: Developing a railway-based ICD. The project will facilitate off-border clearance of cargo.

Estimated Cost ($ million): 100.00

Indicative Funding Source: ADB

SASEC OP: 5

Status: Project planned and funding identified, which may or may not be finalized

Project No. BAN-TF-03

Project Name: Building Capacity in Trade Facilitation

Project Snapshot/Description: Capacity building to support the introduction of modern techniques and the development of specialized centers in the customs organization.

The program components include

i. Strengthening capacity of the Bangladesh Customs Excise and VAT Training Academy;
ii. Strengthening capacity of the directorate of Internal audit and PCA;
iii. Strengthening capacity of the directorates of intelligence;
iv. Support in establishment of national centers on classification, valuation and AEO; and
v. Business reengineering of trade documentation

Estimated Cost ($ million): 1.00

Indicative Funding Source: ADB and Government of Bangladesh

SASEC OP: 1, 6

Status: Project planned and funding identified, which may or may not be finalized

continued next page

Table A6.1: *Continued*

Project No. BAN–TF-04

Project Name: Customs Reform and Modernization for Trade Facilitation

Project Snapshot/Description: To support customs modernization efforts and in effective implementation of the WTO Trade Facilitation Agreement.

The policy-based loan is expected to result in (i) customs legal and regulatory framework aligned with international standards and other best practices; (ii) cargo clearance processes made more efficient, predictable, transparent, and automated; and (iii) trade infrastructure for effective functioning of customs strengthened.

Estimated Cost ($ million): 48.00

Indicative Funding Source: ADB

SASEC OP: 1

Status: Project planned and funding identified, which may or may not be finalized

ADB = Asian Development Bank, AEO = authorized economic operator, BAN = Bangladesh, ICD = inland container depot, LCS = land customs stations, OP = operational plan, PCA = Post Clearance Audit, SASEC = South Asia Subregional Economic Cooperation, TF = trade facilitation, VAT = value-added tax, WTO = World Trade Organization.
Source: Asian Development Bank; country submissions in 2018.

Table A6.2: SASEC Trade Facilitation Projects in Bhutan

Project No. BHU-TF-01

Project Name: SASEC Trade Facilitation National Single Window Project

Project Snapshot/Description: To help the Government of Bhutan develop a single electronic platform to assist private sector activities in operating trade activities efficiently.

Estimated Cost ($ million): 14.40

Indicative Funding Source: Government of Bhutan

SASEC OP: 2

Status: Project planned and funding identified, which may or may not be finalized

BHU = Bhutan, OP = operational plan, SASEC = South Asia Subregional Economic Cooperation, TF = trade facilitation.
Source: Asian Development Bank; country submissions in 2018.

Table A6.3: SASEC Trade Facilitation Projects in India

Project No. IND-TF-01

Project Name: Development of five integrated check posts (ICPs) at selected land borders with Bangladesh, Bhutan, and Nepal

Project Snapshot/Description: Development of five ICPs at selected land borders for more efficient trade flow.

The project covers the comprehensive development of infrastructure at the identified border points to cater to the needs of all cross-border regulatory agencies and trade. In this phase, five locations are expected to be taken up for development. RITES, a PSU of the Government of India has been mobilized to prepare DPRs of ICPs.

Estimated Cost ($ million): 70.00

Indicative Funding Source: Government of India

SASEC OP: 5

Status: Project planned and funding identified, which may or may not be finalized

continued next page

Table A6.3: *Continued*

Project No. IND-TF-02
Project Name: Building awareness of global standards and best practices in trade facilitation

Project Snapshot/Description: Introduction of modern tools and processes to assist Indian Customs in improving efficiency and enhanced trade facilitation.

The program components envisaged are

i. Sharing best practices and knowledge for the implementation of the WTO Trade Facilitation Agreement;
ii. Extending automation to more border crossing points;
iii. Use of electronic cargo systems for off-border clearances across selected corridors;
iv. Improving institutional arrangements for coordinated border management; and
v. Assisting in efficient implementation of the cargo protocol of the BBIN Motor Vehicles Agreement.

Estimated Cost ($ million): 2.00

Indicative Funding Source: Government of India and ADB

SASEC OP: 1, 6

Status: Project planned and funding identified, which may or may not be finalized

ADB = Asian Development Bank; BBIN = Bangladesh, Bhutan, India, and Nepal; DPR = detailed project report; IND = India; PSU = public sector undertaking; SASEC = South Asia Subregional Economic Cooperation; TF = trade facilitation; WTO = World Trade Organization.

Source: Asian Development Bank; country submissions in 2018.

Table A6.4: SASEC Trade Facilitation Projects in Maldives

Project No. MLD-TF-01
Project Name: SASEC National Single Window

Project Snapshot/Description: Effective integration of all the border agencies under a national single window is essential to ensure fast and efficient goods clearance.

Estimated Cost ($ million): 12.00

Indicative Funding Source: ADB and Government of Maldives

SASEC OP: 2

Status: Project planned and funding identified, which may or may not be finalized

Project No. MLD-TF-02
Project Name: Strengthen national quality infrastructure

Project Snapshot/Description: This project aims to establish a mechanism to ensure the safety and quality of the products that reach final consumers, particularly those that are imported.

Estimated Cost ($ million): 16.96

Indicative Funding Source: TBD

SASEC OP: 3

Status: Project planned but no funding identified

MLD = Maldives, OP = operational plan, SASEC = South Asia Subregional Economic Cooperation, TBD = to be determined, TF = trade facilitation.

Source: Asian Development Bank; country submissions in 2018.

Table A6.5: SASEC Trade Facilitation Projects in Myanmar

Project No. MYA-TF-01
Project Name: Building capacity and awareness in Trade Facilitation
Project Snapshot/Description: Capacity building to assist in implementing WTO Trade Facilitation Agreement
Estimated Cost ($ million): 0.50
Indicative Funding Source: Government of Myanmar and ADB
SASEC OP: 1, 6
Status: Project planned and funding identified, which may or may not be finalized

ADB = Asian Development Bank, MYA = Myanmar, OP = operational plan, SASEC = South Asia Subregional Economic Cooperation, TF = trade facilitation, WTO = World Trade Organization.

Source: Asian Development Bank; country submissions in 2018.

Table A6.6: SASEC Trade Facilitation Projects in Nepal

Project No. NEP-TF-01
Project Name: Building capacity and awareness in Trade Facilitation
Project Snapshot/Description: Capacity building to assist in implementing Customs-related WTO Trade Facilitation Agreement and Revised Kyoto Convention General Standards
Estimated Cost ($ million): 2.00
Indicative Funding Source: Government of Nepal
SASEC OP: 1, 6
Status: Project planned but no funding identified
Project No. NEP TF-02
Project Name: Development of Inland Container Depot in Krishnanagar
Project Snapshot/Description: Developing a railway-based ICD
Estimated Cost ($ million): 9.00
Indicative Funding Source: TBD
SASEC OP: 5
Status: Project planned but no funding identified

ICD = inland container depot, NEP = Nepal, OP = operational plan, SASEC = South Asia Subregional Economic Cooperation, TBD = to be determined, TF = trade facilitation, WTO = World Trade Organization.

Source: Asian Development Bank; country submissions in 2018.

APPENDIX 7

SASEC OPERATIONAL PLAN ENERGY PROJECTS – BY COUNTRY

Table A7.1: SASEC Energy Projects in Bangladesh

Project No. BAN-EN-01

Project Name: SASEC Bangladesh–India Electrical Grid Interconnection Project

Project Snapshot/Description: The project will contribute toward efforts of Bangladesh and India to establish cross-border interconnection between the western electrical grid of Bangladesh and the eastern electrical grid of India, facilitating the exchange of electricity between the two countries. This will help address the significant power shortages in Bangladesh. The project only covers the interconnection facilities to be established in Bangladesh.

Estimated Cost ($ million): 199.00

Indicative Funding Source: ADB

Energy Subsector: TI

Status: Project completed or under implementation

SASEC OP: 1

Remarks: The 400 kV AC Baharampur (India)–Bheramara (Bangladesh) line was commissioned in October 2013 and enables export of 500 MW into Bangladesh.

The line has been operational since 2013 and has been providing 250 MW of power from NVVN and 250 MW through power traders to Bangladesh.

ADB financing: $112.00 million

Project No. BAN-EN-02

Project Name: Second SASEC Bangladesh–India Electrical Grid Interconnection Project

Project Snapshot/Description: This project aims to help Bangladesh increase the import of electricity from India to meet increasing power demand, by upgrading the power transmission capacity of the existing grid interconnection between Bangladesh and India from 500 MW to 1,000 MW. Includes installation of an additional asynchronous 4 kV/230 kV MW high voltage direct current (HVDC) back-to-back substation in Bheramara and construction of 12 km of 230 kV transmission line from the Bheramara substation to the Ishurdi substation and associated facilities.

The project has a capacity of 500 MW with 300 MW from NVVN and 200 MW from other traders.

Estimated Cost ($ million): 183.00

Indicative Funding Source: ADB

Energy Subsector: TI

Status: Project completed or under implementation

SASEC OP: 1

Remarks: ADB financing: $120 million

continued next page

Table A7.1: *Continued*

Project No. BAN-EN-03

Project Name: HVDC BtB Station at Cumilla for 500 MW import from Tripura and Assam (India)[a] DPP approved by ECNEC on 29 May 2018 the 500 MW HVDC back-to-back Station at Cumilla North (BAN) for Transfer of Power through Surjamaninagar (Tripura, India)–Cumilla North (BAN)

Project Snapshot/Description: Project aims to meet the growing electricity demand of the eastern part of Bangladesh. It will ensure sufficient facilities to import 500 MW power from India. Scope includes (i) 500 MW back-to-back 400–230 kV HVDC station with associated converter transformer; (ii) 400 kV GIS Switchyard with two line bays and HVDC station connection interface facilities; (iii) extension of 230 kV GIS bays in the existing Cumilla; (iv) 132 kV line bays at Cumilla north substation for terminating of existing Cumilla North–Cumilla South 132 kV DC Line; and (v) termination of Surjyamaninagar (TSECL) – Cumilla (North) 400 kV DC line at Cumilla (North).

Estimated Cost ($ million): 181.00

Indicative Funding Source: ADB

Energy Subsector: TI

Status: Project completed or under implementation   **SASEC OP:** 1

Remarks: Covered under the 2019 ADB project SASEC Third Bangladesh–India Electrical Grid Interconnection. ADB financing: $126.00 million (OCR = $66 million; COL = $60 million)

Project No. BAN-EN-04

Project Name: Interconnection between Katihar, Bihar, India–Parbatipur, Bangladesh-Bornagar, Assam, India at 400 kV DC and augmentation to 765 kV DC

Project Snapshot/Description: Implementation of this line will be in two phases. Phase 1 will involve connecting the three points via a 765-kV DC line to be operated initially as 400 kV, to facilitate export of up to 500 MW into Bangladesh. Phase 2 will involve upgrading associated substations and HVDC terminal from 500 MW to 1,000 MW, including upgrading the Katihar, Bornagar, and Parbatipur substations from 400 kV to 765 kV.

Energy Subsector: TI

Status: Project planned but no funding identified   **SASEC OP:** 1

Remarks: Discussions on this interconnection are ongoing between the Joint Steering Committees of India and Bangladesh.

Interest by Bangladesh will depend on the feasibility of technical options to be studied by Joint Technical Committee (JTT) as discussed in the 15th JSC meeting.

Project No. BAN-EN-05

Project Name: India–Bangladesh Gas Pipeline

Project Snapshot/Description: A 130-km pipeline will connect Siliguri in West Bengal in India and Parbatipur in Dinajpur district of Bangladesh. The capacity of the pipeline will be 1 million metric tons per year. The 6 km Indian section of the pipeline project will be implemented by the Assam-based Numaligarh Refinery Limited and the remaining 124 km of the pipeline project will be implemented by Bangladesh Petroleum Corporation. The project will replace the existing practice of sending diesel by rail covering a distance of 510 km.

Estimated Cost ($ million): 47.00

Indicative Funding Source: Bangladesh Petroleum Corporation (Bangladesh side)

Energy Subsector: OG

Status: Project completed or under implementation   **SASEC OP:** 1

Remarks: Both countries had entered into an agreement for the pipeline construction in April 2018. Cost is $48.47 million.

continued next page

Table A7.1: *Continued*

Project No. BAN-EN-06
Project Name: Natural Gas Transmission Project

Project Snapshot/Description: This will construct about 175 km of high-pressure gas transmission pipeline to expand the country's gas transmission capacity. Project will help meet the gas supply shortfall in the southwestern region and, in addition, accommodate the upcoming diversified gas supply sources from imports and potential offshore discoveries into national network. Executing agency will be Gas Transmission Company Limited.

Project to include constructing 70 km of 36-inch gas pipeline from Bhomra to Aronghata in Khulna district to receive and transmit imported regasified LNG from India through cross-border gas pipeline.

Estimated Cost ($ million): 202.40

Indicative Funding Source: ADB

Energy Subsector: OG

Status: Project planned and funding identified, which may or may not be finalized

SASEC OP: 1

Remarks: Included in ADB's 2020 standby pipeline for Bangladesh as SASEC Gas Transmission and National Grid Expansion Project (Formerly LNG and Gas Transmission Pipeline). Proposed ADB (OCR) financing of $250 million.

ADB = Asian Development Bank, BAN = Bangladesh, COL = concessional OCR lending, DC = direct current, ECNEC = Executive Committee of the National Economic Council, EN = energy, GIS = gas-insulated substation, HVDC = high voltage direct current, km = kilometer, kV = kilovolt, LNG = liquefied natural gas, MW = megawatt, NVVN = Indian power trading company (a subsidiary of NTPC Ltd.), OCR = ordinary capital resources, OP = operational plan, SASEC = South Asia Subregional Economic Cooperation.

[a] Included in ADB 2019 firm pipeline as "SASEC Third Bangladesh–India Electrical Grid Interconnection" for Bangladesh with ADB financing of $126.00 million.

Sources: Asian Development Bank; country submissions in 2018.

Table A7.2: SASEC Energy Projects in Bhutan

Project No. BHU-EN-01
Project Name: Punatsangchhu I

Project Snapshot/Description: This (1,200 MW) run-of-the-river HPP PHEP-I in Wangduephodrang Dzongkhag in western Bhutan is the first project of the 10,000 MW Hydropower Development Initiative taken by the Royal Government of Bhutan and the Government of India to be achieved by 2020. Designed to generate 5,670 million units of electricity in an average year, the project utilizes 357 m head available in about 11 km length of Punatsangchhu.

For Punatsangchhu I, output will be evacuated via two 400 kV lines: one to Lhamoizingkha border, another to Alipurduar HVDC power pooling point in West Bengal.

Estimated Cost ($ million): 1,740.00

Indicative Funding Source: Joint venture with Government of India

Energy Subsector: HP, TI

Status: Project planned or under implementation

SASEC OP: 1, 2

continued next page

Table A7.2: *Continued*

Project No. BHU-EN-02
Project Name: Punatsangchhu II

Project Snapshot/Description: The diversion dam of run-of-the-river 1,020 MW Punatsangchhu II is located about 20 km downstream of Wangduephodrang Bridge. All other project components are situated on the right bank. Its underground power house is 15 km downstream of dam at Kamechu, Dagar Gewog.

For Punatshangchhu II, output will be evacuated via one 400 kV line to Jigmeling power pooling point.

Estimated Cost ($ million): TBD

Indicative Funding Source: Joint venture with Government of India

Energy Subsector: HP, TI

Status: Project planned or under implementation

SASEC OP: 1, 2

Project No. BHU-EN-03
Project Name: Mangdechhu HPP

Project Snapshot/Description: The Mangdechhu hydroelectric project is a 720 MW run-of-river power plant being built on the Mangdechhu River in Trongsa Dzongkhag District of central Bhutan. Mangdechhu Hydroelectric Project Authority, which is constituted by the Government of India and the Royal Government of Bhutan, is developing the project. Mangdechhu is one of 10 hydroelectric projects planned under the Royal Government of Bhutan's initiative to generate 10,000 MW hydropower by 2020 with support from the Government of India.

For Mangdechhu, power will be evacuated via two (2) 400 kV lines: one to Jigmeling pooling point, another to Alipurduar.

Estimated Cost ($ million): 551.00

Indicative Funding Source: Joint venture with Government of India

Energy Subsector: HP, TI

Status: Project planned or under implementation

SASEC OP: 1, 2

Project No. BHU-EN-04
Project Name: 180 MW Bunakha HPP

Project Snapshot/Description: The Bunakha HPP is close to Bunakha in Chukha Dzong, about 3 km upstream of the commissioned Chukha on the Raidak River.

Estimated Cost ($ million): 900.00

Indicative Funding Source: Joint venture with Government of India

Energy Subsector: HP

Status: Project planned and funding identified, which may or may not be finalized

SASEC OP: 2

Remarks: The original detailed project report (DPR) for the 180 MW HPP was prepared by Tehri Hydropower Devt. Corporation (THDC) India Ltd, a joint venture of Government of India and the state government of Uttar Pradesh. The report was approved by India's Central Electricity Authority in August 2013 and was expected to be developed by THDC and Druk Green Power Corporation. Together with BHU-EN-05 and BHU-EN-06 form part of a venture hydroelectric power project (HPP) with India with a total estimated cost of $3,000 million for three projects.

continued next page

Table A7.2: *Continued*

Project No. BHU-EN-05

Project Name: 570 MW Wangchhu HPP

Project Snapshot/Description: The Wangchhu HPP is one of four projects totaling 2,120 MW as part of an India–Bhutan agreement signed to jointly promote hydropower development in April 2014. This project entails a 134 m high concrete dam, with a 12.38 km headrace tunnel and is expected to generate 1,968.55 million units of energy annually.

Estimated Cost ($ million): 1,200.00

Indicative Funding Source: Joint venture with Government of India

Energy Subsector: HP

Status: Project planned or under implementation

SASEC OP: 2

Remarks: Preliminary construction work on the 570 MW Wangchhu HPP has begun. The DPR was vetted by the Central Electricity Authority of India in March 2014 and submitted to the Royal Government of Bhutan in May 2014. The project is a joint venture between Satluj Jal Vidyut Nigam Ltd and Druk Green Power Corporation. Together with BHU-EN-04 and BHU-EN-06 form part of a venture hydroelectric power project (HPP) with India with a total estimated cost of $3,000 million for three projects.

Project No. BHU-EN-06

Project Name: 770 MW Chamkarchu HPP

Project Snapshot/Description: This project is located on the right bank of the river Chamkharchhu, approximately 3.5 km upstream of its confluence with the river Mangdechhu. It includes a 108 m high concrete dam. The Mangdechhu joins the Manas River, which drains into the Brahmaputra.

Estimated Cost ($ million): 900.00

Indicative Funding Source: Joint venture with Government of India

Energy Subsector: HP

Status: Project planned and funding identified, which may or may not be finalized

SASEC OP: 2

Remarks: An intergovernmental agreement has been signed between India and Bhutan through a joint venture between NHPC and DGPC of Bhutan. Together with BHU-EN-04 and BHU-EN-05 form part of a venture hydroelectric power project (HPP) with India with a total estimated cost of $3,000 million for three projects.

Project No. BHU-EN-07

Project Name: Kuri–Gongri 1,800 MW

Project Snapshot/Description: One of the priorities per Department of Hydropower and Power System, Kuri–Gongri HPP is the largest potential contributor to Bhutan's (India-assisted) 10,000 MW target by 2020.

Estimated Cost ($ million): 3,200.00

Indicative Funding Source: Bilateral with Government of India

Energy Subsector: HP

Status: Project planned and funding identified, which may or may not be finalized

SASEC OP: 2

Remarks: DPR is being prepared by the Water and Power Consultancy Service of India, under the Ministry of Economic Affairs of Bhutan. Together with BHU-EN-08 and BHU-EN-09 form part of a new government-to-government HPP with India with a total cost estimate of $9,500 million for three projects.

continued next page

Table A7.2: *Continued*

Project No. BHU-EN-08

Project Name: Amochhu Reservoir 540 MW

Project Snapshot/Description: This project has been planned as a reservoir dam project with hydropower capacity of 540 MW. Given that it is a reservoir project with water storage, unlike most hydropower projects in Bhutan, it will assist in generating electricity in the months when river water flows are low.

Estimated Cost ($ million): 3,150.00

Indicative Funding Source: Bilateral with Government of India

Energy Subsector: HP

Status: Project planned but no funding identified

SASEC OP: 2

Remarks: The original DPR of the Amochhu HPP was prepared in January 2013. Together with BHU-EN-07 and BHU-EN-09 form part of a new government-to-government HPP with India with a total cost estimate of $9,500 million for three projects.

Project No. BHU-EN-09

Project Name: Sunkosh Reservoir 2,560 MW

Project Snapshot/Description: One of the priorities per Department of Hydropower and Power System, the Sunkosh project is part of the ultimate goal of developing 10,000 MW of hydropower in Bhutan by 2020. Sunkosh Project will promote grid reliability by providing ancillary services and high generation possibilities in the winter months.

Estimated Cost ($ million): 3,150.00

Indicative Funding Source: Bilateral with Government of India

Energy Subsector: HP

Status: Project planned but no funding identified

SASEC OP: 2

Remarks: DPR for the 2,560 MW Sunkosh Project is with the Government of India for clearance. Together with BHU-EN-07 and BHU-EN-08 form part of a new government-to-government HPP with India with a total cost estimate of $9,500 million for three projects.

Project No. BHU-EN-10

Project Name: Nyera Amari 442 MW, along with the associated transmission system[b]

Project Snapshot/Description: The proposed MFF will support the development of run-of-river hydropower plant and transmission system facilities in the eastern region of Bhutan, with 442 MW capacity. The power generated from the plant can be supplied through the eastern grid network system for dual purposes of export and domestic consumption. To be developed as public–private partnership. This project will be executed outside the scope of the projects that are identified to generate 10,000 MW by 2020. Once commissioned, the energy will meet domestic demand, and additional supply will be sold to India. The project will contribute to energy security and revenue for the government; promote economic growth and employment; and contribute toward climate change mitigation. In addition, it will promote cross-border power trade and access to clean electricity, contribute to energy sector development and institutional reform, and support public–private partnerships program.

Estimated Cost ($ million): 794.53

Indicative Funding Source: ADB, OCR, COL, COL RCI, COL DRR, COL PBA

Energy Subsector: HP

Status: Project planned and funding identified, which may or may not be finalized

SASEC OP: 2

continued next page

Table A7.2: *Continued*

Remarks: Total MFF ADB financing is $370.53 million; government financing is $144.00 million; and cofinancing is $280.00 million. Overall total: $794.53 million (Bhutan Country Operations Business Plan, 2019–2021).

Tranche 1 (2019) for ADB financing of $123.36 million (OCR – $50.00 million; COL, PBA – $50.00 million; COL RCI – $20.00 million; COL, DRR – $3.36 million). Government – $24.00 million. Cofinancing – $80.00 million (EIB, JICA).

Tranche 2 (2020) for $117.09 million (OCR – $70.00 million; COL – $47.09 million). Government – $20.00 million. Included in ADB pipeline.

Tranche 3 (2021) for $130.08 million (OCR – $870.00 million; COL – $40.00 million; COL RCI – $10.00 million; COL DRR – $6.72 million; DRR financing mechanisms – $3.36 million). Government – $100.00 million. Cofinancing – $200.00 million (EIB, JICA).

Together with BHU-EN-11 and BHU-EN-12 form part of Druk Green Power Corporation's HPP with a total cost estimate of $3,000 million for three projects.

Included in ADB 2019–2021 pipeline as SASEC Green Power Investment Program.

Project No. BHU-EN-11

Project Name: Dorjilung 1,125 MW

Project Snapshot/Description: One of the priorities per Department of Hydropower and Power System.

Estimated Cost ($ million): 1,400.00

Indicative Funding Source: Druk Green Power Corporation

Energy Subsector: HP

Status: Project planned and funding identified, which may or may not be finalized

SASEC OP: 2

Remarks: DPR for the 1,125 MW Dorjilung Project has been completed and submitted to the Royal Government of Bhutan for approval. Together with BHU-EN-10 and BHU-EN-12 form part of Druk Green Power Corporation's HPP with a total cost estimate of $3,000 million for three projects.

Project No. BHU-EN-12

Project Name: Upper Chamkharchhu 556 MW

Project Snapshot/Description: The Upper Chamkharchhu 556 MW HPP project is one of the two dams planned for the river Chamkharchhu. This HPP project, together with Chamkarchhu 770 MW HPP, will constitute the two dams of the Chamkarchhu Integrated project.

Estimated Cost ($ million): 805.47

Indicative Funding Source: Druk Green Power Corporation

Energy Subsector: HP

Status: Project planned but no funding identified

SASEC OP: 2

Remarks: Upper Chamkarchhu is planned to be jointly developed by the National Hydro Power Corporation of India and Druk Green Power Corporation. Together with BHU-EN-10 and BHU-EN-11 form part of Druk Green Power Corporation's HPP with a total cost estimate of $3,000 million for three projects.

ADB = Asian Development Bank, BHU = Bhutan, COL = concessional OCR lending, DPR = detailed project report, DRR = disaster risk reduction, EIB = European Investment Bank, EN = energy, HPP = hydropower plant, HVDC = high voltage direct current, JICA = Japan International Cooperation Agency, km = kilometer, kV = kilovolt, MFF = multitranche financing facility, MW = megawatt, OCR = ordinary capital resources, OP = operational plan, PBA = performance-based allocation, RCI = regional cooperation and integration, SASEC = South Asia Subregional Economic Cooperation, TBD = to be determined.

Sources: Asian Development Bank; country submissions in 2018.

Table A7.3: SASEC Energy Projects in Nepal

Project No. NEP-EN-01

Project Name: Arun 3 Hydropower Project

Project Snapshot/Description: 900 MW run-of-river type hydropower project located on Arun river in Sankhuwasabha District of Eastern Nepal. Surplus power from project to be exported to India.

Estimated Cost ($ million): 881.00

Indicative Funding Source: Private financing

Energy Subsector: HP

Status: Project completed or under implementation

SASEC OP: 2

Remarks: The developer is SJVN Arun 3 Power Development Co. (promoted by SJVN Limited India) under build, operate, own, and transfer scheme for 25 years. Partner is Nepal Ministry of Energy and Nepal Electricity Authority.

Project No. NEP-EN-02

Project Name: Dudh Koshi HPP 300 MW

Project Snapshot/Description: Storage type HPP with installed capacity of 840 MW. Located at border of Khotang and Okhaldhunga districts on Dudh Koshi River in Eastern Development Region of Nepal.

The Ten-Year Hydropower Development Plan, 2008 of Government of Nepal planned Dudhkoshi Storage Hydroelectric Project commissioning in 2018 in order to achieve the national objective of generating 10,000 MW of hydropower over the next 10 years.

Estimated Cost ($ million): 940.00

Indicative Funding Source: ADB

Energy Subsector: HP

Status: Project planned and funding identified, which may or may not be finalized

SASEC OP: 2

Remarks: Detailed design and FS through ADB grant. Developer is Nepal Electricity Authority.

Included in ADB's 2021 pipeline as Dudh Koshi Hydropower Project for $518 million (OCR = $350 million; COL = 168 million).

Project No. NEP-EN-03

Project Name: Nalsing Gad Hydropower Project

Project Snapshot/Description: The 410 MW capacity project expects to generate 1,406 gigawatt-hours (GWh) energy. Includes the approach road up to powerhouse site. Project detailed study was undertaken by consultant. This project is being developed under the Nalgad Hydropower Company Limited to meet the peaking energy demand of Nepal's power system. The project is located in a relatively remote area, so it will help in achieving more balanced regional development.

Estimated Cost ($ million): 987.00

Indicative Funding Source: TBD

Energy Subsector: HP

Status: Project planned and funding identified, which may or may not be finalized

SASEC OP: 2

Remarks: Completed FS.

continued next page

Table A7.3: *Continued*

Project No. NEP-EN-04

Project Name: Upper Karnali Hydropower Plant (HPP) 900 MW

Project Snapshot/Description: Upper Karnali 900 MW hydropower project is contemplated as an export hydropower project with 12% free power to Government of Nepal and 27% free equity to Nepal Electricity Authority. The Project was bid out in 2006 along with Arun 3 hydropower project. The project is contemplated to inject power in Bareilly substation in India interconnecting at Lumki substation in Nepal. Investment Board Nepal (IBN) is the implementing agency.

Estimated Cost ($ million): 1,500.00

Indicative Funding Source: India Private Sector (GMR)

Energy Subsector: HP

Status: Project planned and funding identified, which may or may not be finalized

SASEC OP: 2

Remarks: GMR Upper Karnali Hydropower Ltd. signed PDA with IBN/Government of Nepal in 2014.

Directorate General of Foreign Trade of the Government of India has already granted a long-term license which is valid for 30 years for the import of power from this power project. Completed DPR.

Project No. NEP-EN-06

Project Name: Tamakoshi-V (101 MW)

Project Snapshot/Description: Tamakoshi-V is located in the Central Development Region of Dolakha District of Janakpur Zone, located about 150 km northeast of Kathmandu. This project is conceptualized to develop as a tendon operation project with Upper Tamakoshi HPP.

Estimated Cost ($ million): 150.00

Indicative Funding Source: TBD

Energy Subsector: HP

Status: Project planned but no funding identified

SASEC OP: 2

Remarks: DPR completed.

Project No. NEP-EN-07

Project Name: Nepal: South Asia Subregional Economic Cooperation Power System Expansion Project

Project Snapshot/Description: Project helps Nepal address its urgent power system needs by facilitating expansion of domestic power transmission capacity, improving medium- and long-term power exchange with India, augmenting and expanding distribution networks, and increasing mini-grid-based renewable energy systems in rural areas.

Estimated Cost ($ million): 460.00

Indicative Funding Source: ADB

Energy Subsector: TI

Status: Project completed or under implementation

SASEC OP: 1

Remarks: Total cost includes additional financing. ADB financing = $231.20 million.

continued next page

Table A7.3: *Continued*

Project No. NEP-EN-08

Project Name: Lapsiphedi–Hetauda 400 kV Transmission Line
Transmission Line 1. Kathmandu (Lapsephedi)–Ratmate 400 kV DC Transmission line 2. Ratmate–Hetauda 400 kV DC Transmission line 3. Ratmate–Damauli 400 kV DC Transmission line 4. Damauli–Butwal 400 kV DC Transmission line 5. Butwal–Nearest Indian Border 400 kV DC Transmission line **Substation** Ratmate, Damauli, and Butwal 400 kV Substation

Project Snapshot/Description: Construction of transmission line between Lapsephedi and Hetauda.

Estimated Cost ($ million): 398.20

Indicative Funding Source: Millennium Challenge Corporation (MCC)

Energy Subsector: TI

Status: Project planned and funding identified, which may or may not be finalized

SASEC OP: 1

Remarks: DPR ongoing.

Project No. NEP-EN-09

Project Name: New Butwal–New Kohalpur (Tulsipur)–New Lumki (Dododhara)–New Attariya 400 kV Transmission Line

Project Snapshot/Description: Project will evacuate free energy generated from Upper Karnali HP, being developed by an International firm, and transmit high voltage electricity from central part of Nepal to western part of Nepal. This project includes construction of (i) the 400 kV double circuit New Butwal–New Kohalpur (Tulsipur) transmission line and 400 kV substations at New Butwal and New Kohalpur (Tulsipur); (ii) the 132 kV double circuit Chinchu (Surkhet)–Subakuna (Surkhet) and 132 kV substation at Subakuna (Surkhet); (iii) the 400 kV Double circuit New Kohalpur (Tulsipur)–Chinchu (Surkhet) transmission lines, and 400 kV substation at Upper Karnali; (iv) the 400 kV double circuit Chinchu–New Lumki (Dododhara)–New Attariya transmission lines, and associated 765 kV or 400 kV substation at New Attariya.

Estimated Cost ($ million): TBD

Indicative Funding Source: TBD

Energy Subsector: TI

Status: Project planned but no funding identified

SASEC OP: 1

continued next page

Table A7.3: *Continued*

Project No. NEP-EN-10
Project Name: Augmentation of transmission capacity between Dhalkebar, Nepal to Muzaffarpur, India

Project Snapshot/Description: To augment transmission capacity between Dhalkebar and Muzaffarpur from 132 kV to 400 kV. Currently, 145 MW power is imported from India.

Estimated Cost ($ million): TBD

Indicative Funding Source: Private financing

Energy Subsector: TI

Status: Project planned and funding identified, which may or may not be finalized

SASEC OP: 1

Remarks: Developers are joint venture companies on the Indian and Nepal sides.

Project No. NEP-EN-12
Project Name: SASEC Power Transmission and Distribution System Strengthening Project

Project Snapshot/Description: The project will upgrade existing 220/132 kV substations to 400/220/132 kV substations that would: (i) enable electricity generated from independent power producer (IPP) plants in Khimti HP corridor to be exported to India; and (ii) modernize and reinforce four distribution centers around Kathmandu Valley to be able to meet increasing domestic power demand.

Estimated Cost ($ million): 190.00

Indicative Funding Source: Government of Nepal and ADB

Energy Subsector: TI

Status: Project planned and funding identified, which may or may not be finalized

SASEC OP: 1

ADB = Asian Development Bank, COL = concessional OCR lending, DC = direct current, DPR = detailed project report, EN = energy, FS = feasibility study, HPP = hydropower plant, IBN = Investment Board Nepal, kV = kilovolt, MW = megawatt, NEP = Nepal, OCR = ordinary capital resources, OP = operational plan, SASEC = South Asia Subregional Economic Cooperation, TBD = to be determined.

Sources: Asian Development Bank; country submissions in 2018.

Table A7.4: SASEC Energy Projects in Sri Lanka

Project No. SRI-EN-01

Project Name: India–Sri Lanka 500 MW submarine link

Project Snapshot/Description: Government of Sri Lanka and Government of India have decided to carry out a detailed feasibility study for the interconnection of Sri Lanka–India electricity grids through an HVDC transmission line. During the feasibility study, transfer of 500 MW of power would be considered initially.

Estimated Cost ($ million): 554.00

Indicative Funding Source: TBD

Energy Subsector: Transmission Interconnection

Status: Project planned but no funding identified

SASEC OP: 1

Remarks: Included in ADB 2021 standby pipeline as Preparing Power Development and Interconnection Project (PRF). The initial 500 MW connection will involve 400 kV line between Madurai (India) and Anuradhapura.

Project No. SRI-EN-02

Project Name: LNG Handling Berth and Facilities at Port of Trincomalee

Project Snapshot/Description: An LNG and/or oil handling berth and facilities at Port of Trincomalee could handle the LNG carriers of deep draft without difficulty. A storage tank in the industrial area could introduce a hub terminal for the regional demand for storage and reexport. Sri Lanka's own power needs could be met by a power plant in Trincomalee using natural gas which would yield cheap and clean energy as well as the possibility of trading carbon credits. This requirement is in line with the government policy and ideal solution to meet Sri Lanka's energy demand.

Estimated Cost ($ million): 100.00

Indicative Funding Source: TBD

Energy Subsector: Oil and Gas

Status: Project planned but no funding identified

SASEC OP: 1

Remarks: Sri Lanka Port Authority will undertake infrastructure works of the jetty facility for oil and LNG, while the private sector will operate the terminals. Hence, $100.00 million cost is calculated only for basic infrastructure developments.

EN = energy, HVDC = high voltage direct current, kV = kilovolt, LNG = liquefied natural gas, MW = megawatt, SRI = Sri Lanka, TBD = to be determined.

Sources: Asian Development Bank; country submissions in 2018.

www.ingramcontent.com/pod-product-compliance
Lightning Source LLC
Chambersburg PA
CBHW050046220326
41599CB00045B/7301